The 2 Keys to Business Success

Or

Why an Ounce of Common Sense is Worth a Room Full of Consultants

By

Paul E. Anders, Jr.

Outskirts Press, Inc.
Denver, Colorado

The 2 Keys to Business Success
Why an Ounce of Common Sense is Worth a Room Full of Consultants

Cover Design: Judith A. Anders

Outskirts Press, Inc.
http://www.outskirtspress.com

ISBN: 978-1-4327-5094-7

Outskirts Press and the "OP" logo are trademarks belonging to Outskirts Press, Inc.

Acknowledgements

First and foremost, I need to thank my wife Judy, who listened for years to my ramblings about business theory and often provided me with real insights into how to apply the human factors at work. She also spent long hours reviewing my initially obscure text several times and helping me translate almost every paragraph into progressively more understandable words that would truly mean something to others. Without her ongoing help and encouragement this book would never have been more than idle conversation.

Secondly, I appreciate the help of my two sons Paul and Patrick who were also exposed to my ideas and frequently quipped "You should right a book." Patrick provided many thoughts on the values and audience that the book needed to focus on, while Paul reviewed the manuscript and helped identify the parts that he found particularly applicable to his business environment so they could be enhanced.

Thirdly, to my daughter-in-law and former teacher of communications at the University of Wisconsin Waukesha Campus, Jennifer, for taking the time to thoroughly review my rough draft and apply her expertise to editing the book into correct English.

The 2 Keys to Business Success

Table of Contents

INTRODUCTION

"This Is Where You Decide If You Actually Want To Read This Book."

We live in a very complex and challenging time. Business has become increasingly global and relentlessly competitive. In today's business world the nature of the work force continues to change in a way that demands more and more skill and leadership of the managers that hope to engage that work force. And the compact between business and the employee has been weakened to the point of near extinction in many if not most companies. The task ahead for both current and future leaders is a daunting one if they hope to succeed both personally and on behalf of their organizations and their people.

> **"Managers are necessary, Leaders are indispensable."**
>
> **Anonymous**

I would like to propose that the task of leadership might not be as overwhelming as it appears. I would like to convince you that although there are infinite nuances to the art of leadership, there are a few very straightforward principles that will provide you most of what you need to be successful – thus **The 2 Keys to Business Success.** I would also like to persuade you that these two principles aren't some unnatural, esoteric approaches but rather **common sense** applications of the innate principles that should feel most natural to you. If you read on, I believe I can make your life a little simpler and the success of your organization a lot more likely.

I was academically trained in a strange set of disciplines: a hard science – physics, a soft science - business management, and what some might designate a "voodoo science" - economics. I started my business life as an Industrial Engineer, and then moved into the world of Computer Systems Development and spent over thirty years of my life working in increasingly more responsible positions in the technology realm. But as I moved to positions of increasing responsibility it became very clear that success was 10% about the knowledge of technology and 90% about the science of leadership.

I spent my last fourteen years at the officer level in Fortune 100 companies. I was the Vice President of Information Services for Chrysler Financial Corporation and then the Vice President and Chief Information Officer for Northern States Power, which merged to become Xcel Energy, the eighth largest combined Gas and Electric utility in the United States. I believe that the lessons that I learned in all of that time can be condensed into just *two* key leadership principles. And I also believe that when we dissect these two key principles you will find that most of the logical actions that they suggest just make good sense.

As you read this book I hope that you have a series of "Aha's". That is, the kind of thing that occurs when you read something and then say to yourself: "Of course that's right– it just makes sense!"

I have read many of the major business books published in the last twenty years and I have been to countless seminars by many of the leading practitioners in the business. I have had the privilege of learning relevant business principles and philosophy first hand from brilliant practitioners such as Peter Drucker, Michael Treacy, James Champy, Peter Senge and others. But I still believe that if most of us focus on just two basic principles we will be well on the way to a *successful* business career.

I define success as achieving outstanding results for your enterprise, providing growth and opportunity for your employees and developing career opportunities and continuing challenges for yourself, and doing it in a way that will let you look at yourself in the mirror each morning with pride.

Since I spent most of my business life as a manager and then as an executive, this book is written from the viewpoint of management. It contains a lot of information about how to deal with people. But I believe that the book has appeal to almost everyone in the business world. If you are not yet a manager it will give you insight into how good managers should behave. If you are a beginning leader it will provide you with challenging ideas on how you might be most successful. And if you are already an experienced manager, the book will provide you with another approach to leadership that you can compare your actions against. I believe that every sincere leader will find words in this book that will resonate with good business practices and lead to improved results.

****

This book will provide some simple rules that will help you be successful in your career, but I honestly believe that there are a few other, less serious reasons why you will thoroughly enjoy reading this book:

- First, it is short, so you can read it in one plane trip with some hope of actually remembering what you read.
- Second, it is small, light, easy to carry, and doesn't require batteries – something you'd all like to see in your laptop.
- And third and most importantly it will just make sense to you – *"common sense."*

The concepts presented in this book aren't complex or mysterious. They are based on straight-forward common sense. So why would anyone pay good money for a book that is simply based on common sense? Because I believe that careful observation of both the business place and the world in general will convince you that common sense is a truly rare commodity. It has been obscured by an over reliance on metrics, theory and analysis that are not bad in themselves but that can cause us to make "strange" decisions that in retrospect seldom work out as expected and almost never "felt" right in the first place.

I am not trying to compete with *Dilbert's* creator, Scott Adams, and paint a picture of managers and executives as incompetent. Quite the contrary, I believe corporate America is filled with highly intelligent, committed and hard working people. They don't intentionally act and make decisions in the irrational way that provides the input for Adams' humorous portrayal of the workplace in America. But we live in a very quantitative, analytical world that is becoming more and more complex with each passing day. And I feel that many of us have reacted to this pressure by losing faith in our instincts – in our common sense. And as a result we lose sight of the simplicity of success and make our jobs and our lives a great deal more complex than they need to be.

In fact it seems that we have been taught to ignore common sense. We have learned that it is necessary to carefully analyze **all** of the facts before we come to a decision. We have been instructed to always consult with a host of others before deciding what we should do lest we make a mistake and have to shoulder the blame entirely by ourselves. We have heard the epistle of "empowerment" but yet decisions require consensus and review and revisions and re-reviews. If we don't involve everyone, every time, they won't take ownership of the decisions and then if implementation fails it will be your fault for not obtaining full "buy-in" before you started. This cliché filled process may be valid for the few massive, "bet your company" decisions, but if it becomes the standard for decision making in your company it can paralyze your ability to react to a competitive environment that constantly changes and at an increasing rate of speed.

> "A conference is a gathering of important people who singly can do nothing, but together can decide that nothing can be done."[1]
>
> **Fred Allen**

We have been carefully trained to always seek the help of outside consultants. After all, they have worked with dozens of companies (even if they have only been in the business for a few years) and have accumulated the wisdom of having seen many different variations of your process and been able to witness first hand what works and what doesn't. I am not advocating that every manager should "reinvent the wheel" rather than seek outside help but on the other hand I believe we go too far when we subjugate the unique requirements of our company and put our faith in others to understand and solve our problems for us.

In other words, understanding of the unique culture and practices that define each individual company or organization is often one of the most important elements in formulating effective solutions or plans. Yet this is the area where the consultants have the least knowledge and you and your people have the most knowledge!

We shouldn't sell our instincts short!

7

> **"A consultant is someone who saves his client almost enough to pay his fee."**[2]
>
> Arnold H. Glasgow

On the other hand, this book is not about bashing consultants despite the only half-whimsical sub-title. I have worked with dozens of highly competent, dedicated and productive consultants over the last 30 years. They have performed invaluable services for the organizations that I have worked in, but when and only when their activities were aligned with good common sense practices. By far the best results always occurred when the people inside the company understood well the problems and worked hand-in-hand with the consultants to leverage their talents and knowledge to solve these problem. When internal management abdicates responsibility for the solutions to the consultants, I have seen far more failures than successes.

As we try to make ongoing progress within our organizations, we have been acclimated to the concept that progress embodies change, and change always has some risk associated with it, so is naturally avoided by everyone. This is a strange hypothesis that defies the bookcases full of texts that tell us that change is unavoidable; that good companies encourage "intelligent risk" and reward the risk-takers. All of our companies will tell us how they value people that are willing to innovate and to try new things. Yet the reality is that we have all seen failures punished, even if only passively, and we have to be careful not to let common sense cloud our judgment?! Again we are discouraged from using our instincts; from pursuing the goals that "common sense" defines for us.

The truth is that most of the management concepts proposed in this century have significant merit when viewed logically. But despite our claims to being thoughtful we often tend to rely on the concepts and teachings of the latest author without necessarily using common sense to truly apply them productively in our unique situations. In applying them verbatim rather than thoughtfully we tend to actually diminish the value of the work that careful researchers and very thorough practitioners have undertaken.

The concepts and conclusions published in the ongoing stream of business books almost always have merit in either identifying practices that can be directly applied to our business problems or in introducing concepts that challenge our thought processes and lead us to develop new and better ways of thinking about how to improve our business. However, if we don't integrate these concepts within an overall framework based on our experience and understanding of our own environment, we will significantly increase the risk of either mis-applying the concepts by adapting them to the wrong situations or applying them slavishly even when there is clear evidence that they are not working as expected.

What I will try and do in this compact book is to describe many of the key tenets of management that I have used successfully in my career to guide my work and that I have observed in other competent managers. Then I will simply view these concepts again through the lens of common sense and see what it reveals. And then in the final analysis you will have to make up your own mind about how you believe these principles can be used in your business. If I am right the "sense" of these concepts will ring true and you will just naturally start to apply them and to be more successful. But you must test each of the concepts against your own "common sense" to determine if they are "right" for your business.

You will find a few references throughout the book but not a lot. I am trying to synthesize a lot of information into a core of ideas that will almost always point you in the right direction. But I will provide a short list of books at the end that I have found both enlightening and readable and that you might well enjoy. Some of them are classics and some are relatively new.

You might think of this book as if you were taking Business 202 for your MBA. If you really "buy in" to the concepts presented and try to practice them in your own setting using your own common sense, then

I believe that you will be well on the way to business success. If you find a concept that really intrigues you or that you feel is particularly important, one of the books in the recommended reading list can provide a lot more depth on that particular subject than I am able to do here. But passing this "course" requires you to integrate the concepts of all of these authors and many others into these two simple processes bound together by the glue of "common sense."

By now you may be wondering why you should pay any particular attention to what I have to say. I am not an academic prepared to back up my assertions with detailed statistics, case studies or data gleaned from research studies. I am not a consultant that can claim to have worked with a multitude of successful and unsuccessful companies so that I can offer my insights to what works and what doesn't. I did however, spend over 30 years in management positions at some very large companies. I was a leading advocate of the Quality Movement at Chrysler Corporation. I have worked intimately with IBM, CSC, Delloitt Touche, Arthur Anderson, Price Waterhouse, Microsoft and a host of other major vendors and consultants both large and small. And I believe I am able to describe a set of simple practices that **work!** Certainly they worked for me. I have always tried to drive sustainable change. In the words of the manufacturing guys that were my customers at Chrysler, I tried to create practices that are repeatable. I have tried to create organizations that can survive any leader, merger or other activity because what they are doing feels right to the people, produces results, and just makes sense.

Finally just another attempt to make this book easy and helpful – throughout the text I have tried to summarize key points into a series of **Common Sense Tips.** I have included an appendix that contains all of these tips. So if you really get bored with the book, don't throw it away, just flip to the appendix and you'll be able to learn most of the really important things in a few minutes. But please play fair! Don't just Xerox the appendix and then put the book back on the shelf. I have gotten my teenage neighbor to incorporate a new "copy virus" that will cause the copies to come out in Sanskrit and the copier to spill toner all over your floor --- *and don't be so sure that I'm just kidding!.*

****

This whole book is oriented around what I believe to be the two keys to success in your business or in any endeavor for that matter. The first and most important principle is *"**people**".* We ascribe automatically to this platitude but all too often our actions are not consistent with our words. Strangely enough this is probably because many or most of us don't fully believe the words, or have never made the effort to understand the full magnitude of their meaning. I will try and make this principle so clear to you that you will forevermore think about people first when you are making decisions. The second key principle is *"process"*. This principle isn't as well understood but it is critical to ongoing success because it helps capture the creativity and efforts of the people for the future. The Encarta English Dictionary defines process as a noun meaning "a series of actions directed toward a particular aim." In business a process becomes useful when "a series of actions" becomes defined and recorded so that if it is effective it can be used again by you and by others. Although I fully believe that process is one of the two key principles they are not equal in importance. Process is only a critical tool because it **enables** people to do their jobs better.

****

The First Principle is People

Unless you are the owner and operator of a one-person organization, your success is inexorably linked to your people. If you have four employees then those four people better provide close to 80% of your results. If they don't, you should question why you have them at all. But somehow this truism doesn't seem to reach to the inner center of many managers. They seem to view people as necessary, but not the primary drivers of their success. And in many cases even years of working with people doesn't seem to make them truly understand the power that people bring to the organization's success. Hopefully, this book might be the trigger that helps to clarify these managers' understanding of the value of *"people"*.

> **"One machine can do the work of fifty ordinary men. No machine can do the work of one extraordinary man."[3]**
>
> **Elbert (Green) Hubbard (1856-1915), American Businessman, writer and printer**

Looking back through the record of our experiences should make the facts obvious. It is a well-established axiom in computer programming that your best programmers will produce ten times the output of your average programmers and with better quality. For most of us it only takes a few years of working with people for us to accumulate shining examples of the amazing achievements of our employees and co-workers. Let me provide one from my past:

In 1987 Chrysler Corporation merged with American Motors Corporation, AMC, - remember the Gremlin and the Pacer as well as the Jeep. We had exactly eleven months to integrate the *systems of the two companies or we wouldn't be able to build vehicles in Kenosha, Wisconsin or Toledo, Ohio, which would mean hundreds of millions of dollars in lost revenues. I was the project leader for this effort to integrate the two systems. Over 450 person-years of work was accomplished in eleven months and it all worked. And if you think this was achieved by one person conceptualizing the complete plan and then issuing detailed orders to the other 500 people involved – guess again! It was achieved by establishing a clear and consistent vision of the goal and then getting out of the way and letting the people achieve the objective. It was clearly the **"people"** who created the success.*

In the early eighties I humorously developed a concept that I called the "Burst Theory". The concept is that people achieve the majority of their meaningful work in small "bursts" of productive activity surrounded by long periods of little or no activity. Just think of your own work. You might have an item on your do list for a month. You think about it now and then but never really make any progress. Then, all of a sudden one day, you just feel inspired and you concentrate on that item and it is soon completed and done well. My "theory" postulates that one of the keys to good leadership is to make sure that first, people have the right tools so that during the "bursts" they can achieve the maximum output, and second, to create an environment where "bursts" happen frequently rather than rarely.

I can't emphasize too strongly that positive results don't occur just because the manager is barking out orders. Really meaningful results occur because the people understand the goals of the company and how their work helps achieve those goals. They have consciously aligned themselves with the company objectives because they make sense for both them and the company.

So you see that the first of my *Two Keys to Business Success* is clearly **"people"**. The first section of the book will go on to explain how you need to interact with people to achieve success for them and for you. **They make things happen! They create change! They build success!** Don't ever forget for even a second that they are *Key* to your business success.

****

The Second Principle is Process

The second part of the equation is **process**. Remember that I am talking about a series of steps for accomplishing a goal that are developed, and then if they work, recorded so they can be used again. I became convinced of this during the years that I had responsibility for automobile assembly plant systems. I became very familiar with the concept of <u>repeatability</u>. Even though a vehicle may have a great design and be filled with customer pleasing features, if the assembly plant worker can't put the vehicle together the same way every time without excess effort then the design is worthless – there is no <u>repeatability</u>. Every vehicle coming off the line would be like the reinvention of a car with no guarantees as to quality or functionality.

The quality gurus of the eighties taught an important lesson about defining your processes. You need to develop and document processes so that once you find out how to do something well you can keep doing it the same way over and over again. This lets you focus your creativity on doing new things without having to worry about whether the old things are going to work or not.

This concept applies to every aspect of business. It is similar to a General taking the beachhead in a war. To be successful you have to secure the beachhead and then be able to move on. If you have to keep returning to the beachhead to make sure that the enemy hasn't taken it back from you, then you can't move forward. It is the same in business – you need to identify how to do things well; insure that you can keep doing them the same way; and then move on to other challenges. This also allows you to bring in new or inexperienced people and quickly teach them to be able to perform the defined processes just as well as the experienced people.

So process is the enabler. It frees peoples' creativity by defining the ways to perform the mundane. To use a worn cliché, it prevents people from having to reinvent the wheel. It also helps bring everyone up to the level of the best people. When the best people find a superior way of performing a task you are quickly able to transfer that knowledge to everyone else.

There are just these two key principles and the first and most important is *"people."* I can't emphasize this strongly enough. The people make things happen. They discover and teach the processes. They interpret and achieve the vision. The second key principle is *"process"* which is the key method for helping the people to progress faster and to institutionalize their gains so that they can be quickly shared with others.

So when you put these two key factors of People and Process together into a formula for success what you achieve over time is the following:

- You find and develop excellent people who want to work for your company and are motivated to achieve their goals for both their personal growth and the company's success.
- You provide employees with a clear vision of where you are trying to take the company, or the division, or the department.

- You supply them with the tools, including training and education, to allow them to move efficiently towards the achievement of their goals and your goals.

- As they discover brilliant ways of doing things you record, or document, or in some way "remember" the successful ways of performing tasks so that you can teach them to others.

- You teach the processes to other people who can now progress quickly through the learning curve and soon be ready to move on to new challenges.

- You have your creative, high achieving people, whose numbers are growing all of the time, move on to the next challenge.

I really believe that you can achieve this "nirvana" within your business, of having highly qualified and motivated people conquering challenge after challenge and taking your company or department to ever increasing levels of success if you understand and work on just these two key principles of business success.

****

In the remaining chapters of this book I will explore the details of these two concepts and through *"common sense"* examples provide you not just a blueprint, but a belief system that will make the success that these two principles can provide second nature to you in the future. I will try to help you understand these principles so well that you will never need to reread this book. When situations occur your own *"common sense"* will guide you in the right direction every time.

****

Part 1 - People

Now, if you as a manager, really believe in the concept that people are the first and most critical key to your success then let's look at how to get the right people in the first place; how to retain the right people working for you; and how to keep the right people motivated to continue achieving great things for you – and for themselves.

As a leader you are at the core of this "people" process. Surveys have repeatedly indicated that one of the primary reasons that people leave a job is because they don't get along with or don't respect the person that they are working for. So once again, you need to look at yourself and see if you really believe in people or if you are just riding along with the current fad. Do you really take joy in seeing a team find its way to success or do you just enjoy giving orders and insuring that they are carried out correctly? In the long run, only the first choice is acceptable. If you think that the only way to meet your goals is to just "tell people what you want done" then you have little hope of developing the "**people**" side of the principles. And here is a pretty unpleasant truth – if you don't *really* believe in people, most people will figure it out and they won't want to work for you. You might fool them at the interview time and you might continue to keep them working for you with monetary incentives for a while at least, but you will never get the best out of most of them and given the right conditions they will not hesitate to leave you. A team will walk through fire for a leader they respect and believe in but will only just "punch the time clock" for a dictator they fear.

> **"It is said that a man will work 8 hours a day for pay; 10 hours a day for a boss; 24 hours a day for a cause"**
>
> **Anonymous**

So if after reading this much of the book you are still skeptical, you need to either open your mind to the possibilities of people or you might as well pass the book on to someone else because it won't be of any help to you.

Business 101 – How to Find and Develop Good People
Step 1 – Finding Good People

Let's make the assumption that you have decided that you are at least willing to view these concepts with an open mind. Then the first thing we have to do is to figure out how to find and hire good people. Here is the first, not very big surprise, if you think about it: the most effective way to recruit people is to have your existing people tell their friends, relatives and acquaintances what a great place they work at and what a great person they work for. This method of recruiting wins hands down over every other method for a variety of reasons:

- The current worker doesn't want to bring people into the organization that don't fit or won't work out. That would just make their job harder and hurt their credibility – so they won't tell someone about the job unless they think the person that they are talking to is qualified for the position and even more importantly will fit in with the group. They may not always be

23

the perfect judge of capability and character but they will usually be trying their best to screen the people properly.

- The potential employee also has a trusted source of information about the job. This has got to be far better than a one-hour interview with a stranger or reading about the company in brochures designed to make everything sound wonderful. The prospective employee can make their decision to accept a job based on casual personal discussion and trusted information. Again, they won't always evaluate the information properly and they won't always make the right decision but the odds of a good fit just went way up.

- The potential employee will have a built in mentor in the organization that can quickly "teach them the ropes" and help them deal with the peer pressures of the new work environment.

- Your current employees are performing a highly valuable service when they make these recommendations and you might consider paying them a finder's fee. And for the accountants looking over your shoulder, even if you pay your employee a finder's fee it will be far less than you would pay a recruiter and probably less than it would cost you to recruit through newspapers or on college campuses.

> **Common Sense Tip #1 – Don't make finders fees so high for your employees that they will be tempted to bring in mediocre people just to get the fee. Makes sense doesn't it, but you probably already knew that. The best rewards satisfy people's need for recognition and accomplishment; very few people are only concerned about dollars.**

OK, so your employees continue to refer all of the people that they feel are appropriate but you are in the questionably enviable position of still needing more people – now what do you do? Additional effective methods include internet based job postings, advertising in newspapers and trade journals, recruiting on college campuses, providing clear information about career opportunities and position openings on your web-site, and for some critical or very senior positions using professional recruiters. These approaches may allow you to create a list of possible candidates for your job openings, but the employee referral will still always be your best source.

Step 2 – Convincing Good People to Work for You

After you have found some potentially "right" people, then you bring them in for interviews and here a fair degree of artistry is required along with the continuing application of your common sense; your personal instincts. I won't even attempt to describe the processes that are involved in good interviewing techniques, you can buy a dozen books that will do that better than I can. But I will advise you on how to make the best decision on which people are "right" for the position:

- Be very hesitant to hire a person that you have **any** reservations about. The human chemistry that will make a working relationship effective is far more complex than any interview can ever disclose. The higher the position and the more closely you are going to work with the person the more cautious you should be. The human mind is a far more complicated mechanism than any of us understand and when it sends us a warning we should be very reluctant to ignore it. I know that sometimes we are under a lot of pressure to make a decision but the effort to undo a hiring mistake so overshadows the effort to make the right decision that you should always err on the safe side.

- Put more weight on the person than on their skills. Everyone wants to hire the enthusiastic, experienced employee that has just the right background to step into a job and become immediately productive. If you find that person then by all means make them an offer they can't refuse. Most of the time however, there are compromises to be made and when you have to choose, pick enthusiasm, willingness to learn, and "fit" with your team and your style, over experience and knowledge every time.

During a department expansion in the 70's we interviewed two candidates, Larry and Susan. Larry was incredibly enthusiastic and anxious to go to work immediately, but had only a little experience. Susan was a little odd but had a brilliant understanding of our technology and could hit the "road running."

We weren't too sure of Susan but we sent her to lunch with our best technical experts and they said she really knew her stuff. So we hired both of them. Six months later Susan was gone after having written a half dozen programs that frequently didn't work and were incomprehensible to anyone else. Larry remained a tremendous contributor for years and led the way on

28

several critical projects. Larry's willingness to learn and enthusiasm proved to be far more valuable than Susan's extensive expertise. The person is the key not the knowledge!

Common Sense Tip #2 – The task that you start the person out on will change in a month, a quarter or a year. Then the person will have to learn new skills – so what's more important? What they knew coming in or how willing to learn and remain productive in your environment they were? It's not too hard to answer this question when you think about it that way, is it?

• This is really an aspect of the prior item but it is worth expanding on. If you are really in a bind and need a particular skill set to get a project completed or to get through a tight spot, then hire a contractor that has that specific skill set. This gives you a lot of latitude. If the contractor is the kind of person that you want on your staff permanently you can attempt to hire them later. (Make sure that your right to do this and at what cost is made clear in the initial contract.) If you don't have room for the person or they aren't the kind of person that you want for a permanent employee make sure that they transfer their knowledge to the appropriate people in your permanent staff. (That can be part of the contract as well)

And just an aside about dealing with contract employees. These people can be an invaluable aid to your organization but too often managers feel like they don't need to pay as much attention to the management of contractors from either a performance or a personal side. This is pretty dangerous. Contractors need to be treated like employees in many ways including recognition, challenges and careful evaluation of their work. If you don't track their performance, not only may they feel disconnected from the team but they may seriously jeopardize the team's results if they aren't capable of doing the job and you don't become aware of it until it is too late.

- It is well worth your effort to establish and track goals on the demographics of the people that you hire. Diversity in your work force is a powerful capability and should be a part of everyone's hiring practices, not because it is a legal requirement but because it makes perfect business sense. And that includes diversity beyond the legal definition. Make sure you hire young and old, all races, and all ways of thinking. Your ability to generate new ideas and creative solutions will expand dramatically if you create an organization that can look at the world from many different viewpoints.

- Be absolutely honest about the work, the environment, the career potential and the compensation and benefits. If you lure a person into a job without being 100% honest they will find out what you have done and they will never perform for you the way you need them to.

- Finally don't ever "horse trade" with an employee when you are hiring them. You are trying to create an opportunity that both you and the employee will be pleased about; you are not trying to see if you can get the best "deal" on a new worker. You need to make them the best, honest offer you can and they have to want to work for you at that salary. If you start negotiating back and forth the relationship is done. Either you or the employee will always feel that they got the worst of the deal and you will have established a relationship built on monetary concerns not on trust and a real desire to work together.

This does not mean that you can't consider real concerns in the offer. For example, if an employee is concerned about losing the vacation that they have accumulated in their prior job or if they are worried about losing medical benefits during the transition, you can address those requests to the extent that they are reasonable and can be accommodated in the compensation package.

The interview process is your first real contact with the prospective employee. And my advice is pretty straightforward: Trust your instincts. Look for the future potential in the person. Find people with potential who are willing to try hard and to learn. And then if you want the person, be completely honest with them and give them the best deal you can.

Step 3 - Keeping Good People and Only Good People

Now you have the new employee – a person, not a social security number or an entry in your resource budget. If you think the reason that people work is simply because they get paid well and that's all there is to a productive workforce, you better hire starving people off the street because study after study has shown that money is not the motivator that separates the competent staff from the exceptional one. I know that you have all heard of Maslow and his hierarchy of needs so you know that once people have enough money to satisfy their basic requirements for food and shelter they become motivated by higher needs such as security, appreciation and challenge. But my observations over the last 35 years indicate that many managers do not act like they believe in this progression of satisfiers. They proceed as if a healthy annual raise is all that is required to keep competent people both happy and motivated. In all of my years in management I have never found a single, outstanding contributor who was motivated only by their paycheck. Sure, it is important! If you don't reward people monetarily for the work that they do they will find another job that will. But if **all** you do is reward them monetarily, they are just as likely

33

to find another job where they will be both well paid **and appreciated!**

****

My experience has led me to believe that there are three key elements to keeping good people: honest communications, challenging work and a sincere show of appreciation.

- The first element in keeping good people is **honesty and open communications**. I have found throughout my career that you can never communicate too much information to people. There will always be part of your group, department or company that won't bother to read what you send out or to listen to what you have to say, but the vast majority of the people want to know what is going on and will appreciate your taking the time to try and keep them informed.

  For the last 15 years as head of my organization, I personally wrote a monthly newsletter talking about the key events going on in the company from a viewpoint that was specifically relevant to the people in my department or organization. I discussed organizational changes, the financial outlook for the company, community participation, and the impact of new business objectives.   And I always took every opportunity to recognize good efforts by the employees.

This may seem like a lot of work, but the people told me over and over again that they really appreciated this level of communication and that they wished that everyone they had worked for had taken the time to communicate with them to this degree.   Knowledge gives you power over your environment and helps you make the best decisions for you and for the company.   That is why people are so anxious to know as much as they can about events that affect them.

I also held "skip level" meetings or luncheons with people to try to get the pulse of what is going on at all levels of the organization. (Skip level lunches or meetings are just what the name implies. They are gatherings where you literally eliminate all of the levels of the hierarchy between the workers and the executives.   So for example, the Vice President has lunch with the administrative assistants and the programmers without their supervisors and managers present.)   Even the best-intentioned managers and supervisors create a filtering process when they pass information on to you.   Even if they are completely open they still may try to tell you what they think you will be interested in.   These skip level meetings are a great method for getting a "feel" for the morale of the organization and for identifying the things that are really bothering people.

Be prepared though, these skip level lunches can be tough on you as a leader. By giving people the opportunity to speak to the "boss" you create the expectation in their minds that you will be able to resolve most of their problems. If morale is low you will hear a lot of concerns expressed and in reality you won't be able to magically address all of these complaints. You also have to be *very clear* that this is not a process to bypass or "go around" their normal supervisors. You have a commitment of trust to the directors and managers that work for you that is just as strong as your commitment to the people in the meeting and you have to honor both of those obligations. So be sure that you are very honest with people about what you can and can't do and what you will and won't do. They need to understand that the Skip Level Meetings are just one part of an overall process of open and honest communication that applies to every level of the organization. The Skip Level Meetings are not just a forum to allow them to complain about their managers.

Consequently it is critical that you have a completely open and honest relationship with your direct reports and the managers working for them before you even consider something like "skip level" meetings. If they perceive the meetings as a process to "trap" them or uncover their weaknesses or mistakes – you will do far more harm than good. Trust has to be built at all levels of the organization if it is going to work at any level of the group.

I always tried to summarize the comments made in each meeting without revealing the individual source and then to send it out to everyone in the organization. When we were able to make changes based upon suggestions or concerns expressed in the meetings, I would send out updates to let people see that management was paying attention to their ideas. **Over time this form of communication helps build trust and feelings of self-worth within the employees at all levels and gives them confidence that everyone has a voice in the success of the company.**

Honest and open communication is always the goal that you are striving to achieve with your employees. Newsletters and skip level lunches are efforts to achieve this flow of information. But I understand, of course, that there are times when you will not be able to share things with people. But I believe that these times are few and far between and that unfortunately most managers inappropriately invoke the "rules of secrecy" far too often. When you are legally required to maintain confidentiality you must, and the people who have learned to trust you will understand. When you cannot confirm information that strongly affects people you must either withhold it or strongly emphasize the speculative nature of the information. On the other hand, when rumors are flying around the office about negative events like reorganizations or mergers it is not very productive to simply deny all knowledge of the rumors. You are better off bringing people's concerns out into the open and discussing what you know and what they have heard. In the absence of any information from you, the people will always envision the worst possible scenarios.

Let me insert into this discussion on honest and open communications a few "gems" of homespun logic. I have found these snippets of advice to be accurate almost 100% of the time:

(1) In the absence of real information in a tense situation, the people will invariably imagine the situation to be worse than it is.

(2) If you tell a secret to more than two people it isn't a secret anymore.

(3) And finally the one, which I've found is almost always wrong --- No news is good news.

Sadly a primary reason that open and honest communication is so critical is that people have grown to mistrust most institutions, especially corporations. When a business is going through some kind of change such as a pending merger, the employees will tend to think the worst if they aren't being given steady updates on the activities that are occurring. The idea of keeping a true secret beyond an inner circle of four or five people is almost ludicrous. Especially since any significant information has probably been prepared by other analysts and processed by executive assistants so that there are probably more like 25 people involved in providing the data to the core. When the number gets to ten the odds are infinitesimal that it is still really a "secret." Sometimes you can't help it but under most circumstances you will feel pretty foolish denying knowledge of an upcoming event that your employees are already describing to you in complete and accurate detail. The notion that lack of information is good is about as valid as the idea of an ostrich sticking its head in the sand until the danger passes it by. (Observations have shown that ostriches don't really do that and people need to be at least as smart as ostriches.)

An example from 2000 lends credence to the above concept. At Northern States Power we used the Gallup Q12 Survey to measure employee engagement. This is a survey developed by the Gallup Corporation that asks just twelve questions. But because the survey has literally been taken by millions of people, they have been able to derive highly valid statistics relating the answers to these twelve questions to how engaged the people are in their work. We gave the survey to about 400 people in the Information Technology organization in November 1998 to establish a baseline. And then we administered it again in March 2000 in *the midst of our preparing to merge Northern States Power and New Century Energy to form Xcel Energy. As you can well imagine, this was a very tense time for employees. They literally did not know whether they were going to keep their jobs or not. But an amazing thing happened, the employee engagement scores <u>increased by 20%.</u> When we examined the survey to try and explain this amazing improvement we saw that employees had ranked the department in the 95th percentile on the question that read: "My supervisor cares about me as a person." The lesson was crystal clear. We believe that our effort to constantly communicate with the people is what paid off. We treated the people honestly, fairly and with humanity and they responded even in the most difficult of circumstances. When the merger occurred we were initially able to retain more than 90% of the people despite a severance package that offered some people as much as 18 months of pay and benefits if they left. This is about as clear an example as possible of how to **keep good people** through the use of good communication.*

- The second element in keeping our well-informed, good employees is providing **challenging assignments** that make their work interesting and let them feel that they actually make a difference.

Common Sense Tip #3 – Which would you rather do – go to work or play your favorite sport? A large percentage of people will choose playing their favorite sport. And the reason is because it is interesting, challenging and just plain fun. If we can create that environment at work wouldn't we dramatically increase peoples' motivation and performance?

Obviously not everyone can be on the new and most exciting project, but the management needs to work hard to insure that people's jobs are not drudgery. Most employees want the opportunity to grow by continually learning new things, rotating into different positions, and trying out tasks that they haven't attempted before. Certainly you may have some people who have become very comfortable at doing a particular job and don't relish change in their environment. It is all right to have some of these people if they are truly motivated by their repetitive work, but there are very few people that can't be energized by at least a little change in their environment or their task. And there are very few tasks that can't be done better if some creativity is applied.

In addition to the nature of the work itself, you can also do a lot of things to create an environment that is enjoyable to work in. Make sure that there are plants and pictures, cartoons and photographs. Encourage people to personalize their work areas so that they are comfortable in them. Don't discourage the casual talk in the halls, *unless they are getting together to complain about you.*

The workplace needs to be a place where people can enjoy both a professionally challenging and a socially nurturing environment. Their ability to build close and trusting relationships with their fellow employees will ultimately help them to work better as a team. It will form a discussion platform for them to better understand the goals of the company and how their work fits in. Sure they'll talk about the latest football game or the latest television drama but they will also talk about their latest project, the best techniques for doing their job and a myriad of other things that will directly help them be effective.

Motivated people tend to work harder and smarter. If people are in a rut they quickly learn to utilize just the portion of their mind that is required to get the job done and they save their true potential for their hobbies, outside interests and looking for another job that will challenge their abilities. If you can confront them with new problems and opportunities in their current job, they won't focus their attention elsewhere and you will be another step closer to **keeping the good people.**

- And finally, the third element in keeping our well-informed and challenged employees is understanding that everyone likes to be **appreciated and recognized**. People, especially in professional positions, like to know that they are actually making a difference in the success of the company. Amazingly enough that is exactly what senior management says that it wants. The most effective executives understand that employees need to understand the goals of the company and then choose to work on those things that are most likely to achieve those goals. One of the ways that managers can help make sure that this happens is by creating rewards and recognition that specifically show their appreciation when the people work on the truly important things needed to accomplish the companies goals.

> ..."talking about ordinary people who, given the proper encouragement, can accomplish extraordinary things."[4]
>
> **H. Ross Perot**

However, designing ways to effectively recognize and reward people for their efforts takes us directly back to our discussion on open and effective communications. Recognition systems require highly sophisticated communication processes to be fully effective. One of the common reward systems is an incentive or bonus plan. These systems provide the worker with a monetary reward, usually at the end of the year, based on how their work contributed to the success of the company. This is a very effective way of motivating people but it is also very difficult to do correctly as the following example shows:

Chrysler Corporation, in the late '80's and early '90's had an excellent incentive program. It measured several things including profitability, quality, and market share and it was weighted in such a way as to emphasize longer-term objectives such as quality versus shorter-term objectives such as profitability. It was a great system in principle because employees should have been able to test their actions against the company goals and do the things that would make the greatest contribution. But…It seemed to me, that there were two weaknesses in this incentive system that kept it from achieving its full effectiveness. First, information about where the company stood on the goals was published infrequently and made available to only a few people. So most of the people in the company didn't really know where the company stood throughout the year. Second, the company used a complex *formula to apply **additional** factors to the incentive calculation so that even at the end of the year, when all of the numbers were published it was still impossible to calculate your incentive. The hidden factors could, in fact, have a larger impact on the incentive payment than the employees' actual performance against their objectives. It seems clear that the tighter the link between results and rewards the more effective the incentive system will be. The more communication about where you stand relative to the company goals the more effectively people can focus on helping to achieve those goals – and earn their incentive pay!*

****

Common Sense Tip #4 – If you want people to do their jobs in such a way as to really contribute to the success of your company, doesn't it just make sense that you should give them as much information as possible about how their work is affecting the company and how what they do will specifically affect their compensation?

Another variation of this disconnect between performance, communication and recognition, which many of us have experienced, is the off-balance budget cuts. When a company is experiencing difficulty in meeting its profit objectives clearly you have to increase revenues, cut costs or preferably both. But the approach that many companies take leaves the employees sometimes skeptical as to senior managements' sanity. Admittedly the automobile industry is atypical because it can experience such dramatic swings from profit to loss but it can serve as hyperbole.

Again at Chrysler, in the late '80's when a billion dollar plus loss was anticipated - usually following a year in which the company made a billion dollars, invariably new cost cutting rules would be issued. For example, the company would no longer pay the cost to serve coffee at meetings. The message is clear? The company is continuing its $5 Billion development plan but canceling coffee to save $25,000 a year.

Another example was when Xcel Energy decided that they would close the company cafeteria to save a few thousand dollars that the company paid annually to subsidize the costs of having an in-house cafeteria. As a result, many employees who spent thirty minutes a day having lunch in the building were now forced to spend forty-five minutes or more to go outside to get their lunch and it probably cost them twice as much. This appeared to be a lose-lose situation. The company lost worker productivity far in excess of the few thousand dollars it saved in cafeteria subsidies and the people had to spend twice as much of their own money on lunch.

I am not arguing that actions at either Chrysler or Xcel were wrong. I am just pointing out that management should go out of their way to explain why these seemingly trivial cost reductions make sense especially when they have a direct impact on the employees. If companies don't take the time to justify these apparently arbitrary actions the employees will not understand their purpose and will not support their management's decisions.

Now let's finish our discussion on appreciation and recognition. Everyone wants to be recognized for doing good work or for going out of the way to do a little extra to help the company. Many studies have shown that the key to effective recognition is timing and sincerity.

What people like is to have their boss or their peers notice what they are doing **right now** and thank them for it instead of three weeks later after the assignment is long forgotten. General comments like "nice job" are okay but not enough. You need to demonstrate that you actually understand what the person is working on and the amount of effort required. You also need to be complimenting people for extra effort not just for showing up for work. It is pretty straight-forward – when someone does something special or above and beyond the normal expectations of the job, you need to be right there thanking them for that piece of work. If it is truly extraordinary then you should be thanking them with more than words.

The close link between accomplishment and reward is the reason that ad hoc rewards are so effective. When you say to the employee: "You have really been knocking yourself out to get that proposal done. Take your spouse or a friend out to dinner and a show on us." They understand that you really know and appreciate their immediate efforts. You acknowledge the impact that work has on the employee's personal life and you want to provide a reward that recognizes the impact and bridges the gap between work and home life.

Finding good people is only valuable if you can keep them productive and challenged. In a nutshell, I have described three key elements that will help you to **keep your good people:**

- Make the continuous effort to communicate openly and honestly with them;
- Work to provide them with rewarding and challenging tasks that helps them to grow while contributing meaningfully to the company; and

- Utilize timely methods for rewards and appreciation.

Follow these three rules and your people will follow you.

****

Step 4 - Letting the Not So Good Ones Go

One of the most difficult but most essential jobs of leaders is to keep just the good people. If managers allow mediocre or poor performers to remain the good people will be aware of who isn't pulling their weight in the organization and they won't respect management that allows that kind of inequality to go on. In the worst case the poor performance of some employees will reset the "standards" for the whole department and bring everyone's accomplishments down. That means that you must be prepared to identify the people who just don't fit or don't have the capabilities that you need and then help them to move on. It is clearly one of the hardest but truly the most humane jobs of a manager to honestly assess people's performance and capabilities and communicate the results to them. And just like the old adage states: "Never put off till tomorrow what you can do today." In this case, it simply means that the sooner you identify poor performance the easier it is for you to take action that will be best for both the organization and for the individual.

Just a few pages ago we talked about hiring the person; the person that fits the values of the organization; that will become a strong contributor to the team; that will grow and prosper in your organization. After about six months, you will be able to fit most people into one of three categories: 1) "right on" – this person is well accepted by the group, is growing visibly and is contributing to the company; 2) "bad news" – this person just doesn't fit, they may have great knowledge and skills but they just don't mesh with the values of your company; and 3) "can't tell" – they still seem to be learning and are enthusiastic but the fit with the group isn't clear yet.

Once you have separated the people into one of these three groups, it is pretty easy to determine how you should proceed in each case:

- Group 1 – the "right ons" - Tell them how pleased you are. Make sure they are happy. Look for ways to keep them challenged and growing within the organization. These are your most likely leaders of the future so make sure that you create an environment that will enable their contribution and their job satisfaction to continue to grow. It won't always work out, but they are your best bet so don't leave anything to chance.

- Group 2 – the "bad news" - Don't hesitate. Make sure that other members of your team support your assessment and then counsel them that this is probably not the right place for them. ***There is no reason for you to make this a*** *degrading experience for them.* Emphasize their talents and potential but explain that your organization is not the best place for them. If they are really talented but don't fit in your area look for other opportunities in your company. If they are talented but don't fit with the company culture, give them a good recommendation and help them to look elsewhere.

- Group 3 – the "can't tells" – You can't be sure about these people yet so it isn't time to take either of the above actions. But don't just let them slide. If you can't tell whether they are going to be the employees you imagined, work with them to create a set of specific objectives or expectations over the next 90 to 180 days that will let you separate them into Group 1 or 2 and then take the appropriate action. Then when you know whether they are "right-ons" or "bad-news" you can take the action recommended.

> Common Sense Tip #5 – Quick action is a key to success. It is hardly a life shattering experience to tell an employee of six months that this probably isn't a good fit and that you'll help them find a more suitable job. They probably already realize this isn't the right job for them. But try telling the employee who has been with your company for fifteen or twenty years that they no longer fit. Whose fault is that? These people did what they perceived the company or the department wanted for years and if management failed along the way to upgrade their skills and to keep them challenged shame on management.

When you read this tip you may argue that sometimes people let their skills become obsolete and then they may refuse to upgrade them or be truly incapable of improving them. These are tough cases and the only solution is to deal with it honestly, and openly. Both you and the employee can work together to remedy the situation or they need to leave. You absolutely must do everything in your power to help them to remain employed if they choose and if they are willing to work energetically towards that goal. All of your other people will see how you treat this individual and will judge you by your actions.

****

All of the discussion about **"letting the not so good ones go"** can be distilled to the basics. Just use the Golden Rule – "Do unto others as you would have them do unto you." If you let this be a guideline for you then you aren't going to miss the mark by very much in dealing fairly and humanely with the employees that just don't "work out."

So in theory now, we have an organization that contains the people that we **want;** people that can help make the organization a success. So then how do we develop these "good" people, these "keepers" so that they are constantly growing and improving? **Read On!**

Step 5 - Developing Good People

If you are still with me then let's summarize: we have found good people; we have been able to hire them; and we have practices in place that give us a good chance of keeping them. Now how do we develop these people to their fullest potential? And how do we do it in a way that is both good for the people and good for the company?

Peter Drucker is one of the most respected management practitioners of the Twentieth Century. He cautions us that in the long run people are going to do what they feel is best for them personally. You might be able to get around this if your company has a truly noble purpose like curing disease or rescuing flood victims. If you are in an ordinary business however, you better listen to what Drucker has to say and create an environment that aligns people's personal goals with the company goals and gives them the tools and opportunities to develop their own skills and capabilities.

> **Common Sense Tip #6 – You are just kidding yourself if you think that in the long run people will continue to act against their own self-interest because it is good for the company. Get real – because they won't!**

During a crisis people will behave in heroic, selfless ways. They will amaze us with what they can do and with their capabilities in an emergency but don't expect this to hold true in their everyday work effort. So one of the fundamental keys to developing people is to create a vision of success for the company, which will simultaneously be a vision of success for the individual.

In the early 90's Chrysler Corporation created a simple vision for the company – **To be the best car and truck company in the world by the end of the decade!** *This was an energizing vision. It was a goal that people could and would get excited about. It made you proud as an individual to be a part of accomplishing that goal. And when Chrysler's profitability, market share and reputation began to rise and people perceived the vision as being one they could really strive to obtain it was electrifying.*

Clearly Chrysler lost this vision somewhere along the way and paid a heavy price!

This kind of succinct and powerful vision is a rare occurrence. But you can see the need for this kind of vision that people can understand and make their own; a vision that they will be proud to be a part of.

The next step then is to explore the key steps to aligning objectives and developing people. Individuals will help you achieve the "vision" by creating personal goals. The management challenge is to help them create goals that will be relevant to the company's mission and key components in their own growth.

****

One of the clearest requirements for developing good people is effectively utilizing objectives. Almost without exception any discussion of good management practices will include a section on goal setting. It is almost inconceivable that an organization could consistently achieve success without some clear picture of what it is trying to accomplish. The effective use of objectives requires several key components, namely, **setting objectives, measuring objectives, creating challenge in objectives and recognizing objectives**

achieved. I have utilized processes for establishing clear objectives religiously for three decades but my understanding of what "objectives" means and how to maximize the effectiveness of these tools has continued to change and expand with every cycle. So let's start with an in-depth look at the first of the four points - **setting objectives.**

In 1954, Peter Drucker introduced the concept of Management by Objectives or MBO in his book "The Practice of Management" and we followed his concepts very carefully in the late '70's at Chrysler's Service and Parts Division. The keys to MBO were that objectives had to be realistic, they had to be measurable and they had to contain a timing component. Again this is fairly straight forward. You need to be able to tell by a certain point in time if someone has achieved his or her objectives or not.

Equally important to having objectives that cover a specific time period, are realistic and are measurable is to have objectives that will truly contribute to the overall success of the corporation. Although this sounds obvious it is frequently very difficult to achieve. Often it is very difficult for individuals to see how their personal efforts really make any measurable difference in the success or failure of their company. It is very difficult for the store clerk to see how her friendly demeanor has any real impact on the annual revenue of a corporation that is measured in billions of dollars. And how can you motivate people if they don't see any real meaning in what they are doing or if they feel that the actions of senior management are so overwhelming compared to their actions as to make their efforts meaningless and insignificant.

The automotive assembly line worker is hard pressed to be enthusiastic about being more careful to avoid scrapping a few bolts when senior management is making product development decisions that cost billions. It is even worse if they see the actions of senior management to be in conflict with what they are doing. It is hard for the accounting clerk to be hard nosed about $30 meals on a salesperson's travel expenses when the officer council has just spent a quarter of a million dollars on a planning conference/golf outing at Pebble Beach.

Two key tools that can be used to try and make employee objectives more meaningful are what I refer to as "waterfalling" and utilizing the "wave" approach. The first tool is "Waterfalling" which simply means that the key strategic objectives of the officers of the company are "waterfalled" down to the directors, who set their goals to support the officers' goals. The director goals are then "waterfalled" down to the managers, who set goals to support the Directors' goals. If this is done carefully, then even at the end of the chain there will be a clear link that can be followed all the way up to the highest-level strategic goals of the company. With this process, individuals don't have to be able to relate their goals directly to the overall initiatives of the corporation. Their objectives can be linked closely to the objectives of the next level of management. You can see that "waterfalling" isn't easy. It takes a fair amount of work and careful coordination between each level of management. But if you don't use some technique like this to make sure that individual goals are aligned it becomes almost a random process as to whether any person or manager's goals will actually contribute directly to the Corporation's goals.

David Campbell and Nicolle Hollander wrote a book titled: "If You Don't Know Where You're Going, You'll Probably End Up Somewhere Else. The whole premise of this book is that it takes careful planning if you really expect everybody in an organization to really understand what the company is trying to achieve and how their contribution is important.

The second tool that I am proposing is the "wave" approach. This tool simply recognizes the concept that even the most enlightened Senior Officers of the company cannot set the best goals for the organization without input from other levels of the firm. The goal setting process should exhibit behavior somewhat like waves. Waves (information about corporate goals) flow onto the shore (the other employees of the company), where sand (input from other employees) is picked up and flows out to sea (the corporate leaders) so that the next wave coming into the shore is changed by the new data. Simply put, executives need to listen carefully to the input and ideas of their employees if they really want to be able to set the optimum goals for their company or organization. These leaders will still need to make the ultimate decision but ignoring the input of the people is a risky business indeed.

If we pay attention to these principles we have a good chance of setting objectives across all layers of the company that will actually contribute meaningfully to the company goals. Goals that will truly be a motivator for the people and that will guide their development in ways that will benefit both them and the organization.

So if we are able to use sound techniques to help employees to set goals that are meaningful to them and relevant to the company, then the next step will be to have a process that will let us measure how well the objectives are being met.

****

The next key concept is **measuring and communicating** the results against objectives. I know that it is a well-worn adage that "you can't tell whose winning if you don't keep score." But there is a certain amount of common sense in that saying. If you want people to feel challenged and to constantly improve, they have to know where they stand and they have to know whether their performance is really making a difference.

As I mentioned earlier in the late '80's and early '90's Chrysler had developed a reporting system that was almost ideal in measuring and communicating results against objectives. Chrysler encouraged people to properly align their goals with the company goals and then work hard to achieve the goals by basing a significant portion of management compensation on achievement of the company goals. This "Incentive Compensation" was based on a set of four goals, only one of which was profitability. Other goals were much longer range such as quality and market penetration. There were also secondary measures of things like reputation as a company and as a place to work. Each of these goals had specific numeric targets that were measured and the results were generally published quarterly. So far, I think our common sense would indicate that this is the way we would want to measure and report on objectives.

At year end however, when the incentive compensation was actually calculated, a number of variable controls established by Senior Executives were put in place that made it impossible to determine what your personal incentive was really going to be. For example, there was a published formula for determining how much money would be available for the overall bonus (another word for incentive compensation) pool, but senior management then "arbitrarily" decided how much of that calculated bonus pool would actually be distributed. (By "arbitrarily" I just mean in a way that wasn't explained to lower levels of management; not that there weren't excellent reasons for their decision.) Making 100% of your goals didn't equal getting 100% of your incentive. Even when the results were published regarding performance against the four specific corporate objectives, the incentive payout amounts could vary dramatically because of the unpublished variable factors.

> **Common Sense Tip #7 – Wouldn't it be ideal if a person could plug their individual performance, their organization's performance, the company's performance and the overall profitability into a formula and calculate their <u>actual</u> incentive pay?**

If companies incorporated processes like tip #7 describes, it would not only give you a feeling of real connection to the overall results but of fairness about the whole scheme. I am not sure why so few companies are willing to be this straightforward. But I would propose that there are some pretty "common-sense" rules for good measurement that would result in incentive systems like I describe:

- The measurements must be timely. The point of measurement is to give you information so that you can change what you are doing to improve your results. If the information gets to you so late that you can't use it to make changes in what you are doing in time for the next measurement period then you are forced to figure out some other way to plan your activities.

- The measurements must be focused. If you measure a hundred things people will never understand how to apply the information to their overall job. A few key measurements are clearly the best.

- The measurements must be made known. This is the most puzzling concept of all. In so many companies executives have felt that key measurements must be carefully controlled and only made available to the upper level managers. Pretty silly isn't it. *Keep the measurements away from the people that can improve them.*

As I keep repeating, if you want to retain and develop good people you need to make them feel that they are an integral part of the company. They need to feel that they really make a difference and that *you* want them to have the information to make them successful at their jobs.

Even if we achieve these goals we need to be cognizant of another requirement for objectives that will motivate our people, namely that they need to be **challenging**. We need to think very carefully about challenging our employees. If a goal is too easy, the person doesn't experience real growth. If an objective doesn't challenge the employee it will be impossible or at best difficult to use goal accomplishment to differentiate employee performance and capability. If a goal is too difficult, in most circumstances, people will give up trying.

In the early '90's' Chrysler adopted what I believe was an excellent goal setting process. First, they focused on just four goals for each person. Their approach was to have each employee pick three key goals, that if they were achieved, the person would clearly feel they had an "excellent" year. We were encouraged not to name routine tasks in our goals because they were just an expected part of the job, but rather to focus on the key accomplishments that would really make a difference in the company's results. In other words you wouldn't make one of your three goals: *answer all customer queries within 4 hours,* because that is a routine part of your job. But you might have a goal: *at least 90% of customers will rate my customer service actions as excellent.* Assuming that 90% is an outstanding percentage then this goal might mean real progress for you and the company.

The theory behind this goal setting process made good sense. Executives have dozens of things that they are responsible for and many, many goals to achieve in a given year. If they track their performance against all of those goals the important things become obscured by the mundane and it becomes harder, not easier, to measure performance. So the idea was to pick three goals that if you achieved those goals you would feel that you had an excellent year regardless of how you performed on the other 50 smaller goals that were more a part of your everyday job. I always tried to get the people working for me to try and envision goals in both a rational and an emotional way. I tried to get them to pick three goals that if achieved would give the people a really *good feeling* about their performance for that year.

Then each employee was asked to add a "stretch" goal. Stretch goals had to have the following characteristics:

- The goal had to represent revolutionary change or improvement. A 10% increase in productivity is not a stretch goal – a 300% improvement is.

- At the time the goal is set the employee probably shouldn't have any idea how the goal can be accomplished. The idea is to require "breakthrough" thinking and action. If the goal can be achieved by simply refining existing techniques and practices then it probably isn't a stretch goal.

People were never criticized for not meeting their stretch goals. They were like bonus points, you could still get an A without achieving the "stretch" goal but if you did achieve it or even come close then you could get the A++.

This may sound like a strange goal to you, but my stretch goal for one year was to decrease the average time of meetings from 60 minutes to 30 minutes. If you think of the amount of productive time that is lost in ineffective meetings you will realize that if this goal could be achieved it could have a real impact on the performance of the department and the company. It took a lot of effort and intelligent planning to be able to accomplish the goal of cutting the meeting time in half. Incidentally, I didn't achieve this stretch goal but we did cut 25% to 30% off the average meeting time.

This process allowed people to feel challenged and excited about goal achievement. They focused on the most important and rewarding aspects of their jobs and worked hard to not only maintain good performance but to develop breakthrough ideas. During the early '80's when Chrysler was heavily involved with a quality improvement program the people in my department developed a "stretch" goal around quality improvement ideas. Our department represented about 200 people in an organization of over 1,500 people but while the whole organization did very well our group with its stretch goal was able to implement twice as many quality improvement ideas as the rest of the organizations combined with substantial savings for Chrysler. That kind of achievement is a reward in itself and helps develop and keep good people.

Another way that we stretched ourselves was both fun and rewarding. In the Chrysler quality process, when you achieved certain goals you were supposed to hold a "Defect Free Day" and have a little celebration. One of my very aggressive Project Managers who was helping to plan our "Defect Free Day" suggested that we should invite Mr. Iacocca to attend the ceremony. We all told him to go ahead and try, thinking that Mr. Iacocca would hardly take the time to visit our department. As you have probably guessed, he did in fact attend and we had an outstanding event. Another "stretch" goal that was achieved!

Now that you have worked with your people to establish the "right" objectives – objectives that will challenge them, contribute to the Corporation's success and that are consistent with the value systems of both the employees and the company – what's next?

****

People need **recognition** for their efforts and for their achievements. And they need that acknowledgement not just annually when they receive their incentive check or their annual merit increase, but continually.

Common Sense Tip #8 – If you want to change behavior you need to give clear signals every time the correct behavior occurs as well as whenever the incorrect behavior occurs. Pavlov proved that. After all if the only thing that you reward is the final product, who knows what happened along the way. How many setbacks will people suffer before they give up completely, if the only reward is at the very end of the trail or the project? If your pet does a trick and you don't give them a treat until an hour later it isn't likely that they will understand that the trick and the treat went together. And even though people are a lot smarter than pets the same principle still applies.

Studies have indicated that the most universally desired recognition is praise that occurs almost immediately after the accomplishment of a task and that is given in a sincere and knowledgeable way by the employees' supervisor or their peers. This doesn't mean that the $500 gift certificate at the quarterly department meeting to the top two project leaders is bad it just isn't sufficient. Stop by a few desks each day and compliment people on what they accomplished in their latest efforts. Or give someone a $100 to take their partner out to dinner because they worked all weekend to turn out a successful proposal. These forms of recognition are particularly powerful because they are *personal, unexpected, and sincere.* And don't ever underestimate the value of just saying "good job." *Do it every chance you get.*

And this same logic applies to teams as well as to individuals. Take every opportunity that you can to reward teams. You will almost always succeed or fail as a team but not as a group of competing individuals, and you have to constantly reinforce that truth. The annual incentive plan and merit increases allow you to address people strictly as individuals. But your daily recognition, ad hoc rewards, and interim praise gives you equal opportunity to recognize individuals and to complement the work that people are accomplishing in cooperative efforts, and you don't want to miss these chances. Buying pizza for the team after a long weekend to meet a target or taking them to a ballgame for reaching a project milestone is a powerful incentive to repeat successful efforts.

"Give me a roomful of average people, and you take a room full of geniuses, and my room full of average people working as a team will beat the geniuses every time. Because the geniuses will fight among themselves."[5]

H. Ross Perot

Common Sense Tip #9 – As long as rewards are sincere and equitably distributed you just can't reward people and teams too much. No matter what people say they all like fair and sincere praise.

Step 6 – Training and Educating Good People

So far I have tried to provide some insights into how to attract, hire and retain good people. In the prior sections we looked at ways to help people to set objectives that are challenging for them as well as worthwhile for the company. We have explained the importance and described techniques for measuring their performance. And finally we discussed the necessity of recognizing them for good work every chance we get.

But nothing stays static. So we can't forget that the modern, competitive world will continually present new challenges and obstacles, and making sure that our people are prepared to meet and conquer these new goals can't be left to chance no matter how good the people are.

The key to success in meeting these challenges lies in **continuous learning**. Your people will need to be provided ongoing education and training. You may have noticed that I listed training and education as two different topics. As the discussion proceeds it will be clear why these two approaches to learning are different. The first component of ongoing learning is training. For example, when an Information Technology Organization introduces web based applications into its computer environment people need to be "trained" in some new technologies such as Java and HTML. They need to be taught the "nuts and bolts" of new programming languages and techniques so that they can continue to be effective in developing software for your organization. And this applies to all areas of the organization. It is just as important for the sales and marketing personnel to learn new survey and customer service techniques or for the scheduling department to learn new methods for scheduling production as it is for the systems department to learn new programming languages.

This seems pretty logical, but in fact there seems to be a tendency to believe that ongoing training is only important for the technical areas such as systems and engineering and not as important for the "softer" areas such as human resources and marketing. I would argue that training is critical for every area. No organization or department can afford to keep doing things "the way they have always been done". In today's world your competitors will soon identify a way to provide better customer service or quicker product introduction times and if you don't match or exceed their progress you won't be around. Training is a key to making progress.

Probably most of you buy what I have just said, but you may not be as willing to accept the importance of education in addition to training. Yet I believe that "education" is, in fact, more important than training but often overlooked or considered unnecessary in many corporations. And maybe this is because it is hard to even describe what education means. Here is an example which contrasts training and education. I can "train" a project leader by sending them to a one-week course on using "Microsoft Project" software and they will return with the ability to use a specific tool to schedule and control projects. I can "educate" project leaders by sending them to a one-week session on "Creating positive team dynamics" and they will return with a new mindset that will allow them to build stronger teams across the board regardless of the department which he or she is in.

It should be pretty clear that the potential for "education" to affect the projects success is clearly greater than the potential for "training" to create success. *A high performance team with only average skills in using Microsoft project to schedule and control their efforts will accomplish far more than an average team that is highly expert at using Microsoft Project in support of all aspects of their project – trust me!* Unfortunately many organizations are reluctant to invest in education because it is much harder to measure the result of an educational session than of a training session. You can almost always give people a quiz to see how well they have absorbed a training class, but it is frequently difficult or impossible to test how well people have absorbed an education class. However, in the long term education pays far higher returns than just training.

Later in the book I will talk more about process, what it means and why it is essential, but I want to use system development processes as a telling example here. A "systems development process" is a whole set of rules and guidelines to help developers identify the requirements of a system, define the steps to achieve those requirements and then monitor the development of the system to provide those capabilities.

*In the early 80's Chrysler adopted a methodology called SDM70 (whatever that was supposed to stand for). It described a series of steps that were supposed to lead to the development of high quality systems. Lots of people were **trained** in how to use SDM70 – unfortunately very few people were **educated** in the use of the systems development methodology. The result was cabinets full of excellent documentation following all the rules of SDM70 but very few systems. **Training** left us only half **educated! We knew what to do we just weren't very smart about when to do it and when to stop doing it!***

> **Common Sense Tip #10** – People and organizations either learn and grow or they stagnate and die. There is no in-between. Once you take the hill you need to secure your position and move on to the next hill. If you try to just stay on top of the first hill eventually someone will find a way to knock you off.

****

This section on training and education brings us to the end of the first part of the discussion on people – the more mechanical part. We have seen ways to create an organization that is staffed with good people, motivated to achieve great results that are in-line with the needs of the company, and learning and growing all the time. These are the brick and mortar steps to success.

But even more important is the environment that you create for the people. You can buy some great plants, put them in fine soil, and fertilize and water them regularly. But if they are tropical plants and you are trying to grow them in Alaska, your results aren't likely to be very successful. People are like plants in this way. If they are in an environment that is conducive to their growth and performance they will do well. If they are in an environment, which is inconsistent with their growth and performance, they will struggle to just do average. In this next section on people, we will take a look at the key elements of a fertile environment: trust, empowerment, communication and change management. If you can get these four elements right you will have a great chance of obtaining optimum success for your people and your organization.

Business 201 – How to Create the Environment for

Success

Step 1 – The Foundation: *Establishing Trust*

Trust is the foundation for the development of any effective relationship, whether between team members, or between peers, or between managers and their employees. Trust is a lens by which people interpret the information that flows into them from everywhere. Lack of trust can undermine the most positive message that you try to send while the existence of trust can create an environment of empathy and cooperation that can overcome the most depressing news you convey.

I know that you are reading this and thinking, well of course trust is important. But just knowing this fact is only the barest beginning to actually understanding the mechanisms that can create and maintain that trust. You need to work at it every hour of every day and you need to be sensitive to all of the factors that can affect that trust. You need to be vigilant for the signs that the trust has been violated and you will need to work incredibly hard to reestablish a broken trust.

In the early months of Xcel Energy's formation we believed that we had a relationship of trust with our employees and our key vendor but in 2000 we experienced a mysterious difficulty when the development of a proposal to move a key system from a mainframe platform to a server based platform ground to a halt. Although both the Xcel Energy team and our key supplier both agreed on the solution it seemed that neither side could even come close to agreeing on how to implement the solution or how to achieve the maximum benefits from the solution.

After many discussions, some of them less than pleasant, we finally examined the entire chronology of the decision and the planning process as part of an intensive off-site team building session. And we were all amazed at the assumptions that each side had made about the intentions of the other side. Each side had conceived of the desired solution independently at about the same time and from that moment on each side felt that the other team was trying to take credit for their innovative solution. When the ongoing events were constantly interpreted through that window of mistrust every proposal was viewed as self-serving and to be resisted. When we understood the basis for the mistrust and were able to reestablish the trusting relationship, we were able to move forward on the project.

The misunderstanding that I described above is all too common in the business world but there are tools that can help us to avoid these situations. In the <u>Fifth Discipline Field Book</u>, Rick Ross describes a key conceptual process developed earlier by Chris Argyris called "The Ladder of Inference". This concept recognizes that all information is processed through our own individual "Ladders of Inference". And our "Ladders of Inference" are based on our entire history of cultural influences, overall beliefs, views of the speaker, etc.

In using the "Ladder of Inference" we start with an actual statement or event and then methodically view our understanding of that event through each step of the "Ladder". We start with observable data or actions; then we select information from those observations; add meaning based on our own cultural and personal background; make assumptions based on the meanings that we have assigned; draw our own conclusions; adopt beliefs; and finally we take action. And throughout this whole ladder of inference the only part of the information that could be independently verified is the initial data or actions. Consequently, our conclusion about the intent of an action can vary drastically from the true intent of the action. If our "Ladder of Inference" is based on mistrust then it is almost impossible for us to derive a meaning that is true to the actual intent.

This frequently leads to one of the most insidious forms of performance robbing actions, namely, passive-aggressive behavior. We have all seen this in action. We hold a meeting, get agreement from all of the attending parties on our course of action, proceed with our part of the action, and then find at the status meeting a week later that none of the other agreed upon actions have occurred. And the other parties have very imaginative excuses for why they weren't able to perform their part of the project.

This behavior can destroy almost any project and almost always occurs because there is a lack of trust between the parties. In a trusting relationship the members of the team aren't afraid to speak up and input their own ideas. They are confident that they can comment on the suggestions of the leaders without fear of criticism. They trust that the team will listen and really work to adopt the best approach to the problem and then implement it. In an atmosphere without trust people are afraid to provide constructive criticism; they are reluctant to input their own ideas for fear that they might be used against them.

If people are forced to work in an environment without trust for very long they will withdraw from it in one way or another. Unfortunately your best people will probably just up and leave and find an environment that can more effectively utilize their skills. Other "steady" employees may stay but simply "hunker down" by doing only what they are told, avoiding offering suggestions and analyzing their actions carefully and slowly to insure that they can't be criticized. If you don't understand that this is the result of an atmosphere where trust is missing you will scratch your head and wonder why these good people are so resistant to change and so conservative.

> **Common Sense Tip #11 – If people don't trust you the game is over. They won't believe what you say and you can't tell whether what they are saying is what they really feel or what they think you want to hear. If you are at this point you better figure out how to change it or figure out how to start over someplace else.**

Step 2 – The engine of Productivity: *Creating Empowerment*

In my opinion, in the <u>Principles of Scientific Management</u> published in 1911, Frederick Taylor did the business world of the 21st Century both an enormous favor and an enormous injury. In developing his theories of mass production he introduced scientific method into the workplace and allowed us to achieve a level of output and productivity that could only be imagined previously. In organizing unskilled or semi-skilled workers to perform repetitive tasks he performed miracles that we still utilize today to achieve much of the productive capability of the world.

However, we frequently make the mistake of applying Taylor's principles to a far broader variety of work and workers than he probably ever imagined. In Taylor's world the knowledge and intelligence regarding the work was held in the minds of the supervisors. It was their job to understand and organize the work in such a way that it could be handed off in a repeatable way to essentially interchangeable workers.

But in today's world the strength in most competitive industries is no longer their ability to repeat a specific action in exactly the same way, millions of times in a row. Now competitive advantage comes from being able to react in innovative ways to constantly changing demands. Try figuring out how to respond to every possible variable in a complex environment in advance and then establishing a set of rules for your employees that will predetermine how they should act – impossible!

I have been told that one of the advantages that Japanese Automotive manufacturers have over their American counterparts is in the nature of the contracts that they enter with their suppliers and partners. A Japanese contract is a fraction of the length of an American contract. The Japanese contract attempts to capture the intent of the two parties – it anticipates that they will both act in an honest manner to fulfill the agreed upon intent. The American contract attempts to anticipate every possible problem that could occur and specify the remedy in advance – it assumes that neither party can be expected to act in such a way as to fulfill their obligations. It appears that the Japanese approach encourages innovation and rapid response to changes; the

American approach discourages innovation and can paralyze companies trying to react to change.

In today's environment the manager can't try and think for the employees, the manager has to try and help establish the flow of information to the people so that they can make valid decisions without consulting the leader. The leader has to help define parameters and methods that can help the employees make the best decision quickly when circumstances change. A leader can instill these critical capabilities in his/her employees through the intelligent use of empowerment. But don't mistake effective empowerment as an excuse to abdicate responsibility. <u>Empowerment</u> is not chaos. It is not letting anyone do whatever he or she wants at any time.

Let's take a look at the elements of empowerment. How do we enable people without creating confusion? How do we allow creativity and decision making without accepting wasted time and redundant action? I believe we can achieve effective empowerment through the following:

- People have to be provided with a clear understanding of the goals or objectives of the company and how their work can affect those goals. (Look back at section 5 on developing good people if you have forgotten what I said about this.)

- People have to be provided with a reliable understanding of the parameters in which they can operate. They need to know the kind of decisions that they can make, the resources they can influence and the limits of their decisions.

- Employees need powerful communication systems that bring them information from outside the company about new developments, competitive challenges, new opportunities and threats.

- Workers need strong internal communications about what others are doing and what is working and what isn't working. There isn't time for everyone to make the same mistakes. What works and doesn't work needs to be communicated quickly and broadly.

I'll talk more about GE later under process but their approach to dissemination of information applies here. GE is one of the great US companies. Under Jack Welch they achieved amazing results and one of their key principles was the rapid dissemination of information. Managers were viewed in highest regard if they communicated their good ideas to their peers as rapidly as possible. Keeping a good idea a secret would literally get you fired no matter how well your organization was performing!

- People need to be encouraged to experiment intelligently and boldly. They must be rewarded for valid attempts even if they fail. **No action is far worse than intelligent failure.**

"It is better to attempt too much than to try too little."[6]

Lee Iacocca "Iacocca a Biography"

"The more we keep ourselves in the same place, the more leaks will spring in the boat that wasn't rocked."[7]

Dr. Sonya Friedman

Common Sense Tip #12 – When a team or an individual attempts something new the organization learns whether the attempt is a success or a failure. If people continue to do only what they know is safe and will work, they inevitably will fall further and further behind the competitors who do extend themselves to try knew things. Inaction results in certain failure – there is nothing worse!

- People have to be told when they are operating outside of the bounds of their authority and responsibility.

These steps will create the environment for an empowered work force. And if you have the right kind of people they will produce surprising results if they can operate in this environment. But it isn't easy to achieve this kind of environment.

Especially in today's world, the expansion of knowledge in every field is daunting. No individual manager or executive could ever hope to remain current on all of the changes. Think how foolish it would be if you promoted your best technician to a job as a department supervisor in 1997 and seven years later you still expect them to be not only a great department supervisor but also still your best technician. If they spent enough time to stay the most technically expert then they wouldn't have time to perform the leadership functions that empower the current group of skilled technicians.

Empowerment is the engine that powers your organization. Your job as a leader is to enable your people to utilize their full knowledge and capabilities to get the job done. You can certainly utilize your experience and knowledge to help them — that is part of the communication process. But if they are waiting for you to tell them what to do you are in big trouble. Remember "The Burst Theory" that I talked about earlier. Empower them with the right tools and the right information so that they can fully utilize their energy and creativity to accomplish the company's goals. When they feel that "burst" of energy to achieve their objectives make sure that they are fully empowered to make it happen.

Almost every organization in Western Civilization will quote some slogan like: "People are our most important asset." Many of them don't realize how true this statement is. People are the human computers of the organization. They have within their minds the data for decision-making, the rules for processing the data, and most importantly, unlike any computer they have an amazing creative capability that allows them to utilize the data in unique ways to generate new ideas, new products and new capabilities. They can fully achieve these capabilities only if you are truly willing to empower them to do so.

Step 3 – The Fuel for Success: *Insuring Good Communication*

Business writers frequently counsel us that you simply can never communicate too much. I think that there is more truth than hyperbole in this statement. In the last ten years I have surveyed the people in my organizations six times. And although the overall survey results have ranged from good during troubled times to excellent at other times, where there have been indications of dissatisfaction the root cause in every case has been lack of communication.

Now your first reaction might be: "well this is pretty simple – you just need to communicate more with your people." However, for the last two decades I have tried to be the most ardent of communicators. I have shared every possible bit of information with the people. I have personally written and e-mailed to every employee in my organization weekly or monthly newsletters. During most of that period I held some form of skip level lunches on a bi-weekly basis. In the last four years I had lunch with every employee in my organization, about 400 people, at least twice. And despite this effort the surveys continued to indicate that the people wanted more communication. At the same time, when you talk to people they will tell you that they are overwhelmed with the amount of information that is coming to them and frequently they don't find the time to read all of the communications. This points out just how difficult effective communication can be – people **want** more information but complain that they don't have time to review it.

People need to know what is going on. They especially need you to trust them with all of the information that affects them, including information about the company, the industry, competition, changing policies, etc. But they need it presented in a way that doesn't waste their time, in a way that lets them easily find the information that is important to them. *When you withhold knowledge of events that specifically affect the people involved, you better have a solid legal or competitive reason that they will understand when the information is eventually revealed, because if you don't, then they won't believe what you tell them in the future.*

Another key finding in my experience occurred about ten years ago at Chrysler Financial when we were working closely with the Benchmarking Institute of America. We decided to actually benchmark our communications processes. So we formed a cross-functional, cross-hierarchical team and worked carefully with the *institute to benchmark what we believed were already pretty effective communications processes. The results came as a real surprise to us. What we found when we surveyed people was that they felt that the communications between management and the employees was fairly weak — not because management wasn't making a significant effort to communicate with the employees but because management wasn't **listening** to what the employees had to say. It was a sad observation of our management team because like too many other management teams we were surprised by the fact that communication needs to be **two way**. It should be pretty obvious that if you want to provide the information that people really want and need, and if you are really interested in answering their legitimate questions you need to listen to what questions they are asking in the first place.*

Effective communication revolves around the four key points introduced above, namely, frequent communication, concise information, trusting people with information, and listening to what they have to say. Here are ways that I found effective in implementing these four concepts:

- Make your communications personal whenever you can. I will repeat my earlier story about the Gallup Q12 survey of employee engagement because I believe that it again offers indisputable evidence of the power of communications.

We used the Gallup Q12 survey to measure employee involvement at Northern States Power. We took a survey in the Information Technology department in November of 1998 and scored a somewhat disappointing 46th percentile. In March of 2000 we took the survey again and scored in the 66th percentile.

At the time of the second survey we were in the midst of both a merger and a complete outsourcing of our function and yet we scored twenty points higher than in the previous survey. So in the midst of significant uncertainty and fear our scores improved dramatically. We found the explanation in one of the questions: "My supervisor or someone else in the organization cares about me as a person." We scored in the 95th percentile on that question. In other words, despite all of the uncertainty, people felt that we were all in it together – and that made all the difference in the world. At this time with the merger pending the company was sending out intranet bulletins on a regular basis to keep people informed about what was going on with the merger. And I was also writing a separate news bulletin every time a general message was sent out explaining what the news meant to the people in my organization and how it might affect their jobs.

The measurable results of this effort – less than 2% attrition during the merger period, better than 90% acceptance of job offers to remain with the company, and better than 90% acceptance of job offers to transfer to the outsourcer; all of this despite the fact that the people were given severance packages that could range up to 18 months of pay. In other words, people had the golden opportunity to take 6 to 18 months of pay and go find another job or stay with the department and take a chance on the newly formed company and the vast majority of people stayed.

- Try to be as concise as possible. At the same time that you are trying to insure that all of the important communication is occurring, there is no doubt that people are simply overloaded with information. So try and make your information appear frequently but as compactly as possible. Tell people exactly what is happening and what they need to know to interpret it but don't add on a lot of commentary.

- Don't keep anything secret unless it is absolutely required for legal reasons. Things start out as confidential information between a few people who are required to know. In my experience when that number grows to about ten people, the game is over. I can't count the number of times that I have been embarrassed to feign ignorance with my direct reports when they come to me with the accurate details of an ongoing transaction or process or organizational change and I am required by executive management to claim that I don't know the facts. They know, that I know, that they know .... Pretty silly, isn't it.

- Don't stretch the truth or try to protect people from the truth. Always be honest when you communicate with your employees or anyone else in the company. People would much rather know exactly what is going on and as soon as possible. You need to make this a concept throughout all of your communications.

We emphasized this honesty in the process we utilized for measuring our progress against major projects, which we called the MARC Report. MARC stands for "Milestones Achieved and Required for Completion". We broke every major project into the key milestones and measured each milestone against time, cost and functionality. If any milestone slipped behind in any category we turned it yellow immediately and forced a plan to be developed for how the milestone would be restored to green. This process almost assured that even the best of projects would sometimes go yellow or even red – but the honesty of the process insured that the right attention and action plans would be developed to get the project back on track. This is in sharp contrast to the all too common process where problems would be hidden for days or weeks while the team tried to resolve them before admitting them to anyone. It is too often the norm in this situation for the problem to progress so far that it can't be remedied before anyone is aware of it.

With the honest communication process inherent in the MARC report the results were impressive. With eight major projects under way simultaneously, representing over $130,000,000 in capital expense, all of the projects were on time and on budget. At that time our CEO expressed the opinion that the I/T department of the newly formed Xcel Energy was probably pursuing the most aggressive implementation of computer systems ever undertaken by any utility company and we were doing it successfully.

- Get out amongst the people as often and in as many ways as you can. Don't pass up any opportunity to meet with people on their turf, to learn what the requirements of their jobs are and to get to know every one of your people as individuals. People work for people – not for positions. If you are real to them they will want to do their best for you. I remember telling people at a skip level lunch that I sometimes felt uncomfortable walking around the department and just talking to people. I felt like they would think that this was just an artificial process to show an interest that wasn't really there or to check up on them because in an organization of over 400 persons, I just couldn't keep track of what every employee was doing. They always assured me that whether I was uncomfortable or not I should keep visiting them. The people liked to talk about what they are doing and they really appreciated the opportunity. They assured me that they enjoyed the interaction and the more I did it the more natural it would become.

Common Sense Tip #13 – Don't you know from your own experiences with your family and your friends that you are always anxious to do your best for people that you are close to and that you enjoy working with and being around. Doesn't it just make sense that it would be the same with the people that you work with? Sure they will work for financial rewards and advancement, but if they are also working because they enjoy and respect the people that they are working with, they will just naturally do better.

****

Communication is the most important fuel in the engine that creates success for your company, your organization and of course for the people in the organization. You have to do it often; you have to use many forms; you have to do it honestly and sincerely; and you have to listen as well as talk. So to steal Nike's phrase "Just Do It!" Without good, honest communication there can be no empowerment, no valid objectives, no trusted performance appraisals or company metrics. So make communications a constant priority in your efforts.

Step 4 – The Road to Real Improvement: *Enabling Change*

> **"Faced with a choice between changing one's mind and proving there is no need to do so, almost everyone gets busy on the proof."[8]**
>
> John Kenneth Galbraith

Change is a confusing concept. We are led to believe that change is the key to success but that all people resist change. And the popular press is in equal confusion.

Johnson and Blanchard produced an amazing best seller called: <u>Who Moved My Cheese?</u> It has been on the business bestseller list for so many years that it is most likely familiar to the great majority of you. This book is all about change and why it makes us uncomfortable and why so many people resist change both in their daily lives and in the organizations that they are a part of.

Mark Milleman published a book in 2000 called: <u>Surfing the Edge of Chaos</u>. In his book he makes a compelling case for the fact that in both nature and in business growth occurs "at the edge of chaos." In fact if natural systems or businesses live or operate in a very stable environment for too long and are then faced with a dramatic change – they seldom survive. They have literally forgotten how to change and so when change is necessary, they die, or quietly fade out of existence.

So what is going on here? Doesn't the old adage say, "Variety is the spice of life?" So why does the common wisdom tell us that people are afraid of change and will just naturally resist change when it occurs?

In fact it has been my experience that given the right conditions many people love change and welcome new challenges. They don't want to perform the same comfortable jobs day in and day out, they want to learn and grow and do new things. And guess what – they happen to be your most valuable people. At the same time there is no question that there are people who are threatened by change. And if you look carefully at your corporate environment you may be able to see why. Does your corporation truly reward innovation and intelligent risk taking? Or does it either openly or subtly punish people who take a chance and fail?

Every major change will have risks associated with it. The very nature of change is that it is introducing new and unknown requirements into the environment. People will have to take some chances in a changing environment. They will have to make some guesses. Obviously if they try to keep applying the same old rules and practices in the new environment they will be guaranteed failure.

So are you creating an environment where people will be excited about the opportunity to apply their experience and knowledge in meeting new challenges, confident that you and the company are supporting them, that you are expecting them to make a few mistakes but to achieve great results in the long run? Think about this analogy for how you approach change. Do you present changing requirements to your people like it is a test that they will either pass or fail? Or do you present it to them like a difficult puzzle that they will enjoy unraveling. A puzzle that if they don't get it quite right the first time they will still learn from doing it and have a higher probability of getting it right the next time.

> **Common Sense Tip #14 – Change isn't all that scary if you are all in it together. Most people are more than willing to explore new things along with a group of friends even though they would be reluctant to try them on their own. It is the same in business – implement change together as a team and it will produce amazing results and people will embrace it not fear it.**

Organizations have to grow in two ways if they are going to survive. One way – the way of Deming, the famous quality guru, and many others is to continuously improve the processes and methods that they are using. You need to get a little bit better every time you do something – because your successful competitors will do just that and leave you behind if you don't keep up with the race.

The other way - touted by Michael Hammer, James Champy and others, is through revolutionary or discontinuous growth. This is the way of real change. Where you leap ahead of your competition, at least for a little while, because you and your people have embraced not just a small incremental change but a major revolution in how you do your business; or maybe even in what your business is.

One of the most often quoted examples of this discontinuous change involves the digital watch. It was invented by Swiss watch makers and presented to the management of their companies. (At the time, Swiss Watch makers had an 80% share of the high end watch market.) The management rejected the idea of a digital watch as something no one would want to own. Within fifteen years the digital watch, manufactured and marketed by Japanese and other countries had decimated the Swiss Watch industry taking away 80% of their business.

You can read all about the science of change in other books but your organization must learn to embrace change or it will not survive.

****

This section on change brings us to the end of the second part of our discussion about people. You can clearly see that the second section requires far more creative attention from you than following the more mechanical rules of the first segment. The four concepts of trust, empowerment, communication and change management are key to creating the right environment for your people. If you can do this right then your people will grow in confidence and capability at an astounding rate. And the thing that will insure your career success is that while they are growing they will be accomplishing amazing things for your company at the same time.

A Final Word about Part 1: People

I hope that what you have read so far has come across as mostly
common sense and that the simplicity of the first part of this book has
struck a melodic chord in your mind and in your heart. *People really are
the key to everything.* They bring new thoughts and ideas to your
organization at the same time that they execute the well-tested routines
of their job. They can do this with enthusiasm and commitment that
focuses their full energy to improving your company, your
organization and themselves. Or they can plod along following the
rules and wishing that they were somewhere else doing something else.
How you lead and manage them is the critical element in which way
they will view their jobs and their future.

It is crystal clear that people working with enthusiasm and
commitment will produce so much better results for the company and
for themselves. And the way to create this environment where the
people will be energized should be equally transparent. **Treat them
like people.** Trust them, communicate with them as often and as

111

openly as possible, and truly appreciate their unique and wonderful capabilities. You can accomplish this in a lot of ways so that the actions fit naturally with your style and personality - some managers might display great empathy for their people while others may be very abstract in their approach. But whatever approach is natural for you, you better find a way to reach the people or there is almost no possibility that you can maintain high performance in your organization for any length of time. If you can build this foundation around people then you can move on to processes, which will further enable the capabilities of your employees.

****

Part 2 - Process

The second key to business success is **process.** Dictionary.com defines **process** as a noun meaning: "a systematic series of actions directed to some end." In the business world process is exactly that; typically a documented or recorded series of steps to accomplish some goal. And in the context of this book **process** is an enabler for the **people** to achieve their objectives.

People want to do good work. They want to have challenges and they want to be creative but you don't want them to spend all of their time re-inventing the wheel. However, frequently when we introduce the concept of process, people will feel that their creativity is being stifled in the name of efficiency. So convincing them that **process** is good for them is the tricky part and it takes some selling to get people to understand what you are trying to help them achieve. You need to get them to understand that if they utilize process to perform the routine, they will free up their time to create new opportunities and new approaches that advance both them and your company.

For almost thirty years I worked with computer analysts and programmers. And for those of you who have done the same you know that they don't usually like methodology, they are suspicious of standards, and they definitely don't like documentation. Their frequent argument is that you are interfering with their creativity. Here is where you need to be clear and compelling. Methodologies and standards are simply **processes.** They aren't intended to limit creativity at all. Processes are valuable because they make the simple stuff routine and as a result the people will then have time to focus their creativity and intelligence on the hard stuff. For example, you need to convince programmers that taking the time to create a new routine to edit social security numbers when a standard routine already exists is simply a waste of time. They need to spend their time creating new systems that don't already exist rather than reinventing ones that already do.

However, we have to be careful not to take reliance on processes too far. If we let processes start to replace common sense the results can be pretty undesirable. In the early 1980's I was responsible for introducing a systems development methodology into Chrysler. (A systems development methodology is a formal set of rules and guidelines for the step-by-step analysis, programming and documentation of a computer system. In other words a formal **process.**) By the end of the 1980's I was helping to get the methodology **out** of Chrysler! Here is the practical lesson.

In 1985 I took responsibility for Chrysler's manufacturing plant systems and was reviewing the systems under development. One team told me that they were right on target for developing a new material control system for the manufacturing plants. I asked them where the system stood. They showed me three 3" binders of system design documentation. I asked them when the system was scheduled to launch. They told me in about two years. I asked why so long. They said they hadn't started to write the code yet!

--- I felt more than a little responsible for creating what seemed to be a big problem, since I was responsible for introducing the methodology they were now using. The people were following the methodology slavishly and were measuring their success not by the contribution that they were making to the company but by the number of pages they were filling out in accord with the methodology.

As the above story demonstrates, if you aren't careful people may stop thinking and become overly reliant on processes to define their jobs for them. That is not the intention! The intention is for the processes to support routine efforts of the people and to free their creativity so that they can achieve true breakthrough results and not just replicate old results in new ways. Process is an **enabler** for the people. This is one of the reasons that I preach the importance of always thinking of the people first. If you forget that and let process take the dominant position in your strategy for success you run the risk of letting the process get in the way of the peoples' productivity. They will either resist the process because they feel that it interferes with their originality or they will be over reliant on the process and let it suppress their own unique thinking.

This poses the question again of why have processes at all if it leads to complaints or misuse. The reason is that process has several positive aspects. It helps create repeatability in jobs so that people of different experience and skill levels can produce acceptable results. It helps provide training for new people who can follow the established process. It can help people to complete the routine parts of their job quickly so that they have more time to work on the areas that they find more enjoyable and that produce more important results for the company.

Common Sense Tip #15 – No company can afford to have people spend their time figuring out how to do things that others have long since determined the best way to do. So use process to get the easy stuff out of the way and personal creativity to make a difference. Once you figure out the best way to balance your checkbook you wouldn't try a new way each time just to exert your creativity.

Business 301 - How to Build Processes that Enable Success

Step 1 – The "Gimmee" of Process: *Eliminate Waste*

The first big benefit of process is the elimination of waste. This is the "easiest" process because the elimination of waste produces value by having you do **less** work. During the late 70's and early 80's America became obsessed with quality and process redesign. Many brilliant practitioners wrote about the productivity gains that could be achieved through the application of quality and process redesign concepts. One of the things that all of these practitioners, from Deming to Hammer, had in common was that the typical organization was wasting a huge amount of time by doing things that just aren't worth doing.

Phil Crosby, one of the highly successful quality gurus of the '80's, wrote in his book "Quality is Free", that he estimated that the average company was probably wasting 40% of its efforts on doing things that just didn't have any real value. And you don't even have to search very hard to find examples of this waste in the everyday business world as this story illustrates:

> *One of the most often repeated and dramatic examples of waste elimination has to do with computer generated reports. (In the "old days" the reports were printed on giant high speed printers locked away in computer rooms. In today's world the reports come off of laser and ink-jet printers on practically every workers desk. But the problem of too much paper has gotten worse not better – so this example is still relevant.) At Chrysler we printed copies of every report that the company generated and laid them all out on tables in a huge meeting room. We then asked managers and executives to review all of the reports and indicate which ones they still wanted to be printed and distributed. At the end of the review period half of the reports hadn't been identified as being currently needed by anyone. So we were literally wasting half of the paper, ink, file cabinets and desk space in the organization to print information that nobody even looked at. **If that isn't a clear example of waste I don't know what is!***

This is just one example that challenges us to explore what are the things that we do that actually bring value to the customer and what are the things that we do just because we have always done them? How many reports generated within business are never looked at, or just glanced at and thrown away? Or worse yet, how many reports are filed without even being looked at which not only wastes the resources to compile them but the resources to store them? How many meetings are held when an e-mail or phone call could have accomplished the purpose just as well? And how many analyses are compiled when the information really needed to make the decision was already available after the first analysis? And how many times are consultants called in, which delays decision making and significantly increases costs, when the knowledge necessary to make the decision already existed within the company. All of these efforts are made with the best of intentions but waste time, money and effort because they aren't based on truly rational processes.

We have all probably heard the stories of regular weekly reports that were inadvertently missed because of a computer error and no one ever noticed they were missing. Think of all of the areas where this kind of waste can occur.

- Does our internet site have 100 web pages, when only 25 are ever accessed?

- Are we generating 100 page reports where people only look at one or two lines?

- Are we creating data entry programs that span five screens when one or two would do?

- Are we equipping customer service representatives with so much information that they can never find the relevant section to help the customer?

- Are we scheduling meetings for an hour that only need to be 15 minutes?

- Are we inviting 10 people to a meeting that could be handled with 3?

- Are we producing and distributing information that is out of date by the time it reaches the customer so that they can't use it?

- Are we performing function after function just because we have always done it that way?

All of these things are producers of waste. They use computer resources, office supplies and most importantly, they waste peoples' time in creating the information and storing it. Even ignoring the information takes peoples' time. And all of these time wasters are incredibly hard to stop. Try getting a department to stop sending you a report that you no longer need. Try getting your web master to delete half the web pages on their favorite site even though nobody looks at them. Or try getting someone to stop printing a report of information that is readily available on-line. Frequently you will give up in exhaustion before you are able to actually get the paper to stop coming or the number of web pages cut in half. Try cutting in half the number of people that you invite to meetings. You will typically hear cries of people being left out and slighted. Although these same people will complain equally about how they don't have any time to work because they are always in meetings.

And the key to waste elimination is frequently just the use of good processes. If we critically examine the inputs available and the outputs desired we can often design processes to make the production of those outputs efficient, reliable and repeatable. We can develop a process for determining how and when to conduct meetings and who should be invited. We can identify what information is valuable and what is the best way to generate and distribute the information. Process is a key enabler in the elimination of waste in your organization. Process can identify the importance of incoming information, the value and understandability of resultant outputs and the efficiency of the methods used to generate the outputs.

Common Sense Tip #16 – Try doing a time study on yourself every year or so. (By the way that just means keep track of how much time you spend on each task during a day.) A lot of you won't want to take the time to do this or will think that it is silly. However, I did this every two or three years throughout my career and always found the information to be highly revealing. I was always able to look at the way I was spending my time and identify ways to eliminate things that just didn't produce much value. Like everyone else you are probably wasting 20%, 30% or even 40% of your time. So maybe you will agree that it is worth an investment of a few minutes of your time on a study that might save you at least an hour a day from then on?

The most wasteful thing that you can do is to work hard to produce a great product that nobody needs. The best way to eliminate waste is to just stop doing things that don't provide value. This immediately makes your life both easier and more fulfilling and allows you to focus on activities that will bring true satisfaction to you and true value to the company.

Start here. If you don't get any farther, try to identify things in your job and your workplace that you can just stop doing. This is another valuable aspect of the "waste" process. You can do it yourself for elements of your job day in and day out. Or you can do it as part of a team for processes big and small, complex and simple and always get the satisfaction of making everyone's life easier and everyone's job more productive.

In your attempts to identify waste, your common sense will be your most important tool. Think about the amount of time and effort that you put into each task and the resulting value that it brings. You should see some fairly obvious anomalies. You will find that you are spending a lot of time on some reports that nobody ever seems to actually reference. You will find that you are keeping track of some things that just don't mean much. You will find that you are spending an inordinate amount of time on certain functions and that there is no visible output. There have been some very formal techniques published that will allow you to examine major processes and refine them but those techniques are beyond the scope of this short book. However, I believe that you can make a significant personal start if you just take time to think about what you are doing and how you are doing it.

Step 2 – Keeping Score: *Creating Effective Control and Measurement*

When we talk about people we must recognize the value of being able to measure their efforts, and processes can provide significant help to your people in establishing and maintaining controls and metrics. (Metrics is just a fancy name for measurements. That way I don't have to use the same word every time.) But you will have to be a salesperson extraordinaire to convince them that all of this is good for them. People will feel that "controls" are a way of limiting their freedom and creativity and that "metrics" are a way of building a case against them so that you can give them smaller raises and lay them off whenever you feel like it. (There is a bit of neurosis in all of us.)

Once again I have to go back to the people side of the equation. We talked in the earlier sections of the book about "trust". It is a cornerstone of everything that you are trying to accomplish and it is particularly important at this point in the use of processes. If your people don't trust you it will be a more than Herculean effort for you to convince them that any of the controls and measurements that you want to implement are in their best interest. So first think about the level of trust in the organization. If the people don't believe in your integrity then go back to the earlier section on "Trust" and work on how you can build that trust. Without establishing this basis of trust you are wasting your time trying to implement the metrics part of the process because the people will just report what they think you want to see. They will distort the measurements. And they will figure out how to get around the controls.

There are two ways to try and establish controls and one way is a lot more likely to work than the other. The first way is to try to edit, or inspect every action that your employees take. For example, in a loan department you can set up a system to check every credit application that the employee enters to make sure that every entry meets some pre-determined criteria set by management. The second way is to establish clear directions, trust the people to follow the directions and randomly audit the results to see if there are any problems. In this second case, you audit one out of every hundred credit applications entered to insure that people understand the rules and are staying within the established parameters. *These two approaches produce very different psychological responses.*

In method one, people actually feel challenged to figure out ways to "beat the system". And their fellow employees often secretly applaud them for outsmarting management. In the second method you have trusted people to do the right thing and if an audit reveals that they have been making a mistake they will regret their error because you have shown faith in them and they will want to live up to that expectation. In method one you have demonstrated explicit mistrust and the employees will act that way. In method two you have demonstrated explicit trust, and the employees will again act according to your expectations. Which way would you like to be treated?

Common Sense Tip #17 – If you treat people like they can't be trusted then they will behave that way. And if you treat people like they can be trusted then they will prove you right. Which way would you rather be treated?

Now assuming that you feel that there is sufficient trust in the organization to allow you to proceed, let's talk about controls. Controls are intended to do a number of things:

- Help people avoid wasting time doing things that aren't part of their job or that don't provide any real value to the organization.
- Help people avoid wasteful overlap with other departments.

- Help people keep activities within certain previously determined ranges, which have proven to provide the best results.

- Help people avoid inadvertent decisions or errors that could adversely affect the company.

Controls are not intended to do other things such as:

- Limit people's creativity.

- Prevent employees from trying out new ideas and techniques.

- Limit communication between employees.

- Covertly catch people in mistakes and errors.

To be successful in the implementation of controls you have to be thoughtful in their design. One of the most important things that you can do is to get the employees fully involved in the design and implementation of the controls. Self-directed small teams of employees that work on process improvements and controls for their own jobs are usually more effective than anything else.

I remember attending a seminar at the Ford Motor Headquarters in the 80's. The speaker discussed the success of employee suggestion systems in the United States Automobile industry versus the Japanese Automobile Industry and although the exact numbers have long since escaped me the message has *remained crystal clear. In the U.S. for every ten automotive employees the company received one suggestion a year. Committees would review the suggestions and about half of them would be approved and implemented with each suggestion providing an average value to the company of $5,000. In Japan the average automotive company employee turned in ten suggestions a year. 90% of the suggestions were implemented and they provided an average value to the company of $200. At first blush it looks like the U.S. is way ahead at $5,000 per suggestion versus $200 per suggestion. But let's just assume there are 100,000 employees in each company and do the math:*

- *US – 100,000 X 10% X 50% X $5,000 = $25,000,000*

- *Japan – 100,000 X 10 X 90% X $200 = $180,000,000*

It is obvious that getting full employee involvement pays big dividends. Additionally if the employees design and implement the controls themselves they will help to monitor each other rather than forcing management into a policing role, which will hurt trust. And not only does this help with the establishment of good processes but it makes the people feel more trusted and valued which contributes to their remaining with your company.

When you have the people involved in designing the processes that will help them improve their own job performance then you can assist by giving them guidance in performing the actual process redesigns. (Again books by people like Michael Hammer can provide detailed information on what a process redesign is and how to conduct one. But in general a "process redesign" is a formal approach to trying to develop a better way to do an existing job.) Once again I would draw on my past experience to strongly recommend that you keep it simple. Over the years my management teams arrived at a formula that produced excellent success for us after trying different process redesign methods for years.

We would spend one and a half days off-site defining the current process. Then we would spend the next day and a half designing how the future process should work. Then we almost always found that there would be some missing facts and some questions to be answered so we would break for a week or two. People would be given assignments to gather information and to bring back data. Then we would meet for another day and a half and we would finalize the new process and the implementation plan. We almost always found the results of these sessions to be positive. They were focused and understandable and the people were able to achieve real and rapid results.

This may not make a lot of sense to you. But Chrysler Corporation was really into the more traditional process redesign. A process redesign of the vehicle marketing process had been established that spanned every aspect of the process from the time that a car was available for purchase from the factory until the time that it was delivered to the final customer. This process redesign went on for <u>several years</u> and literally involved hundreds of people. A lot of dramatic improvements resulted from this approach but it also exhausted the energies of a lot of people and took years to implement compared to the more focused and much faster process I describe.

I am not trying to dispute or replicate the work of many excellent authors on how to do process redesign. There are certainly situations where much more formal and extensive process redesigns are justified. However, I am just trying to emphasize that when you focus on areas that can be addressed in a four and a half day process redesign a number of good things happen:

- People remain energized and enthusiastic – three or four straight weeks in process redesign sessions can get awfully tiring.
- People get to see rapid results from their work, which gets them excited.

- People learn what works and what doesn't and they can apply that quickly to the next design effort.

And obviously these are all good things.

Common Sense Tip #18 – If you want to try out the effects of a new drug you test it on fruit flies or mice, not elephants. By using fruit flies you can see the effect on 100 future generations in a year whereas you wouldn't even have the second generation of elephants at the end of the year. In other words, if you act quickly, then assess the effectiveness of your actions, and then act again you are a lot better off than if you spend a huge amount of time on your first effort and find out it didn't work the way you wanted it to. You might not ever get enough energy to even start the second effort.

Okay, so far we have been focusing on controls, so now let's attack the next topic, namely, metrics. And once again there is an almost universal praise for the value of measurements and at the same time a universal aversion to actually using them on the work that you are doing. Similar to controls, in general the key element is trust. Metrics can be used to help people achieve their goals and obtain satisfaction and rewards. Or they can be used to highlight errors and criticize people for not reaching their objectives. You have to insure that they are used as a positive motivational factor or it will never work.

Just as with process controls, one of the most straightforward keys to successful measurements is simplicity. You can quickly fall into any number of traps in developing good metrics. Here are some of the most common:

- The measurement is so difficult to obtain that the cost of measuring the results is more expensive than the potential improvement in the results. (Your elaborate system detects fraud accurately in one out of every 10,000 billings but the cost of the system far exceeds the amount of fraud detected.)

- The metric attempts to be so precise that it can't be taken at frequent enough intervals to be meaningful. (The Gross National Product, GNP, for example has so many variables applied that it can only be issued quarterly and then it has to be revised the next quarter.)

- There are so many different measurements that it is impossible to act on all of them or even to tell which ones are relevant. (For example you measure 50 different variables that affect buyer preference for new cars and then can't correlate the data to determine which variables really make a difference.)

- The metrics are pretty good but they aren't taken on a timely basis so by the time the measurements are available it is too late to act on them. (The monthly overtime report is generated the 15th day of the month after the overtime is worked. What are you supposed to do then?)

- The measurements are good and timely but they aren't distributed to all of the people that need to see them. (The long distance phone call report is sent to the communications department rather than to the department heads that could actually act on the information.)

All of these traps generally occur because we have made the measurements so complex or ill-timed that they no longer provide useable information to people. In the vast majority of cases the precise measurement is not nearly as important as the trend.

Common Sense Tip #19 – if you are dieting and you weigh yourself every day it isn't really very important whether your scale is in exact alignment with your doctor's scale. What is important is that if your scale tells you that your weight is going down, it really is! What I am trying to say is that most of the time the exact measurement isn't as important as the trend.

The obvious key here is to keep it simple. John Rockhart developed the concept of Critical Success Factors or CSF's in the early 70's. One of his key concepts was that you had to focus on the **Critical** Success Factors, which should only be three to five for an entire company. That is all that you can afford to focus on. In developing objectives with my people I have always encouraged them to limit themselves to three objectives. I told them to use the criteria that if they accomplished those three objectives this year they would consider it a good year regardless of what else happened. Obviously this is an oversimplification, but the message is that there are lots of day-to-day things that we have to make sure get done. But we want to focus our creative attention on the few critical things that will really make a difference in our success. (If this sounds familiar we talked about it under people too.)

Our simple measurements need to have a few key characteristics:

- They need to be relatively easy to obtain.
- They need to be timely enough to support action.
- They need to be understandable to everyone that uses them.
- They need to be visible.

If you follow these few key ideas you can readily establish a set of metrics for your department or group or organization that will have real meaning and that can drive activity to achieve your objectives. In my organization of nearly 500 people at Northern States Power we posted three objectives: one that measured customer satisfaction, one that measured cost effectiveness, and one that measured timely work completion. And I don't mean that we had numbers for twenty-three different projects and cost figures for twenty-seven budget areas. I mean that we posted **three** numbers on a chart that everyone saw and understood. I strongly advocate that once you have decided on your measures you either put them up on a big chart on the wall or you put them on your department intranet site so that they are the first thing that people see in the morning when they log on to the site.

****

There is an old adage that says "you can't tell if you're winning, if you don't keep score." It is equally difficult for individuals, or departments or whole companies to know if they are achieving their goals if they don't have good metrics to measure their progress. The section we just finished tries to instill the importance of simple, honest and timely measures as a key process in the success of your organization. People want to "win" and they can "win" in the organization by having measurable goals and then watching their progress until they meet or exceed those goals. Did you ever see a charitable campaign that didn't set a goal and then put up a big chart, usually a thermometer, to show how they are doing against the goal? As long as we make our measurements a relevant way to measure our success and not a way to punish failure they will be a critical element in our success.

****

Step 3 – The Natural Result of Process: *Enabling Change*

The final topic that we need to talk about under processes is change. This can be the natural enemy of improvement or the catalyst that makes it accelerate. We talked about change at the end of the section on people and how it is critical to growth and even survival. Change is a natural result of process and you can use it as a litmus test to see whether your process efforts are successful or not. If process is being used in your organization as a bastion against change then you have a problem. If people are quoting directives, methodologies and procedures instead of thinking, then process is being badly misused. If people are filling out forms and completing pre-designed documents without any thought to the applicability of the information then you have gone astray.

Process, if we use it properly, can be both our anchor and our compass. It can create repeatable methods that allow certain rote work to be performed quickly, with less training, and with more precision day in and day out. You can order a McDonald's hamburger anyplace in the United States and it will taste the same because it will be produced as a result of a very specific process regardless of whether the cook has been on the job for two days or two years. Process can result in good training materials that help bring new people up to speed quickly. It can provide good reference information to resolve daily problems or techniques to help identify the methods for solving daily problems. And most importantly, process can quickly point out the areas where good methods don't exist to deal with new and changing problems. Process can clearly anchor us firmly in the known and point us in the most likely direction to weather the unknown.

Change is a hard topic to write about because it is almost like a religion. You have to have faith that change will take place and that in the long run change will move us continually towards better ways of doing business, better ways of experiencing personal growth and better results for the person, the department and the organization. If you can really internalize this belief then it will guide you to a set of actions that can make change occur naturally and effectively. It will create fervor for inventiveness and intelligent risk.

Intelligent risk? What exactly does that mean? In some organizations the fear is that the only intelligent risk is one that results in success. But of course the real meaning of intelligent risk needs to have three specific components.

- First, the estimated costs and the potential benefits must be examined up front so that we aren't over-investing in projects that simply don't have adequate promise to justify the risk. We want to be equally sure that we aren't bypassing projects with significant potential based on some absolute level of risk tolerance. In other words the more you have to gain the more you might be willing to risk.

- Second, the project needs to have carefully established milestones and measurements to assess its progress and its ongoing potential for success. By far the biggest failing in industry is not that they try too many risky projects; it is that they fail to stop projects long after it has become clear that they aren't going to be successful.

- Third, every project needs to have clear learning outcomes. It is all right for a project to fail, hopefully early on and with limited cost, but it is not all right for a project to fail with no learning derived that can be applied to improve the chance of success on the next project.

Now, if you think about the guidelines above, doesn't *intelligent risk* make good sense? You risk resources in relation to the potential gain, you monitor progress carefully to prevent runaway costs, and you insure that you learn from both the successful and the unsuccessful projects. Sounds pretty **intelligent** to me.

✶✶✶✶✶✶✶✶✶✶✶✶✶✶✶✶✶✶

Another aspect of change that can spell the difference between company growth and stagnation is the method and rate of dissemination of changes. General Electric under Jack Welch was fanatical about the distribution of ideas and the transfer of new methods. People were rewarded for "stealing" ideas from others and putting them into practice. If an executive was ever found to be hoarding an idea it was considered a mortal sin. If you look at the annual reports for General Electric over a ten year period you will be amazed at their ability to disseminate ideas into their operating units around the world. General Electric would hold periodic meetings to bring operating heads together from business units all over the world with the express purpose of sharing information. This was clearly a key element in their success.

And this brings us again to the holistic nature of this whole discussion about **people and process**. If you have created an organization where there is trust, support, excitement, and enthusiasm for growth then dissemination of new ideas is a snap. People will want to help others succeed and to share their ideas and their successes. But if you have created an organization where there is mistrust, secrecy, and fear then people will not want to share their new ideas. They won't mention any new ideas until they have become successful. That way they will get all of the credit for successful innovations and none of the potential criticism for failed experiments.

Common Sense Tip #20 – It should be clear that you are better off with ten good ideas that are quickly dispersed throughout your company than with 50 good ideas that are selfishly hoarded within a single department. Not only will the ten ideas result in improvements throughout the organization but they will also continue to foster an environment that nurtures good ideas and trust between all employees and departments. The ten good ideas will surely spawn additional thinking as they are understood by others throughout the organization, which will result in the birth of even more good ideas. While the ideas hoarded in one department will only spawn mistrust.

One last aspect of change that needs to be addressed is the rate of change or "speed". In 1990, Stalk and Hout published a book called Competing Against Time. This book proposed a simple principle that I believe to be true. Stalk and Hout proposed that you needed to focus your attention on a single key aspect of your business and they believed that if you focused on time, then cost and quality would follow. Remember this was in the hey day of process redesign. They put forth data that indicated that if you could cut the time to complete a task in half you would save 15% of the cost and improve quality at the same time. This was based on the fact that prior to process redesign there were a lot of wasted and redundant actions in processes that both increased the cost and introduced the potential for errors into the process.

There is a great lesson to be learned from the concepts presented in Competing Against Time. In implementing change or running a project you have a lot of talking and planning; followed by a series of actions; and then hopefully you obtain some results that are measurable so you can tell if you are actually achieving what you set out to do. I propose that speed is of the essence in implementing change and needs to be accomplished in two ways.

- Break the process or the project up into as many logical milestones as possible with measurable results for each milestone. That way you find out two weeks or a month into a project if you are on track not a year and a million dollars later.

- Get to the actions part as quickly as possible. Planning is very important and not to be ignored but often it is possible to initiate clear actions while the overall plan is still being developed. This lets you move rapidly towards milestones which both check the progress of the team and energize it as it achieves interim goals

Change is scary because it introduces so many unknowns into the equation. But if you can segment change into a number of small, easy to understand, quick steps it just won't be as intimidating. People will be much more likely to take small risks for short periods of time than to take big risks that won't prove out for months.

Common Sense Tip #21 – Isn't it pretty clear that whether you are trying to achieve small incremental changes or large revolutionary changes that they are going to be a lot easier to sell in small chunks. We have at least 50 clichés to remind us of this. For example: The longest journey begins with a single step.

A Final Word about Part 2 – Processes

Process is the second part of the equation for success. Without good processes you are hard pressed to repeat the successes that you achieve because you have to keep learning to do things all over again. Your new people don't have any history to teach them the most effective way to do things and your experienced people are wasting too much time relearning methods that have already been established. Also if you don't codify any of your processes then what your department or organization learns stays within the minds of just a few people. But if you do record your successes through the use of processes then they can be distributed throughout the organization and the company.

Process is the way you "patent" your people's good ideas. It records them for future use and protects them, not from others, but from being forgotten. It establishes the base of knowledge that others can build upon to keep discovering increasingly effective ways to accomplish their goals and to conceive and conquer more ambitious objectives. Process will streamline the routine and unlock the path to creativity and growth

In Conclusion

So, was the time that you spent reading this book worth it or would you have been better off creating another spreadsheet on your laptop to analyze the buying patterns of your customer base? The latest spreadsheet might give you some insight into how to approach your next customer but I would hope that the time you spent reading this book will give you some insight into how to approach the rest of your business career.

I hope I have been able to demonstrate a way to make the extremely complex job of leading a small or large group of people not as daunting as you might think. Those people are almost always trying to do what is right for the company and what is good for their career. And if you use just the two principles described in this book you can help lead them in the best direction.

In this book I have tried to show you that most of the time you can make the right decision by just thinking about a problem and then using your **common sense**. If you do the things that **seem** right; the things that you would like people to do to or for you. Guess what? A high percentage of the time they **will** be the right things. If you let your intuition measure your actions against core values like trust, integrity, and confidence in people you will get the response that you expect and desire.

> **"Whether you say you can or whether you say you can't – you're right!"**
>
> **Attributed to Henry Ford**

****

So now all you have to do is have at it! Because the whole concept of this book is simplicity and common sense, you should be able to begin tomorrow. Do the things that make sense and see how people react. My 30 years in management tell me that you will see positive results almost every time. Use appendix A if you are ever stuck. It will provide 21 common sense tips that will energize you to find a hundred more on your own. If something isn't working exactly as you expect in your particular situation then just use your own intuition to change it a little and see if it works better.

****

People make things happen and make life enjoyable. Treat them with
trust and respect and they will surprise you with their
accomplishments.

Process helps people to be more effective. Use it intelligently and
simply and it will increase the productivity of your people every time.

And temper it all with your own **common sense**. It will serve you
well if you have the courage to believe in it.

Appendix A
The Tip Sheet

Finding Good People -

Common Sense Tip #1 – Don't make finders fees so high for your employees that they will be tempted to bring in mediocre people just to get the fee. Makes sense doesn't it, but you probably already knew that. The best rewards satisfy people's need for recognition and accomplishment; very few people are only concerned about dollars.

Convincing Good People to Work for You -

Common Sense Tip #2 – The task that you start the person out on will change in a month, a quarter or a year. Then the person will have to learn new skills – so what's more important? What they knew coming in or how willing to learn and remain productive in your environment they were? It's not too hard to answer this question when you think about it that way, is it?

Keeping Good People and Only Good People -

Common Sense Tip #3 – Which would you rather do – go to work or play your favorite sport? A large percentage of people will choose playing their favorite sport. And the reason is because it is interesting, challenging and just plain fun. If we can create that environment at work wouldn't we dramatically increase peoples' motivation and performance?

Common Sense Tip #4 – If you want people to do their jobs in such a way as to really contribute to the success of your company, doesn't it just make sense that you should give them as much information as possible about how their work is affecting the company and how what they do will specifically affect their compensation?

Letting the Not So Good Ones Go -

Common Sense Tip #5 – Quick action is a key to success. It is hardly a life shattering experience to tell an employee of six months that this probably isn't a good fit and that you'll help them find a more suitable job. They probably already realize this isn't the right job for them. But try telling the employee who has been with your company for fifteen or twenty years that they no longer fit. Whose fault is that? These people did what they perceived the company or the department wanted for years and if management failed along the way to upgrade their skills and to keep them challenged shame on management.

Developing Good People -

Common Sense Tip #6 – You are just kidding yourself if you think that in the long run people will continue to act against their own self-interest because it is good for the company. Get real – because they won't!

Common Sense Tip #7 – Wouldn't it be ideal if a person could plug their individual performance, their organization's performance, the company's performance and the overall profitability into a formula and calculate their <u>actual</u> incentive pay?

Common Sense Tip #8 – If you want to change behavior you need to give clear signals every time the correct behavior occurs as well as whenever the incorrect behavior occurs. Pavlov proved that.

After all if the only thing that you reward is the final product, who knows what happened along the way. How many setbacks will people suffer before they give up completely, if the only reward is at the very end of the trail or the project? If your pet does a trick and you don't give them a treat until an hour later it isn't likely that they will understand that the trick and the treat went together. And even though people are a lot smarter than pets the same principle still applies.

Common Sense Tip #9 – As long as rewards are sincere and equitably distributed you just can't reward people and teams too much. No matter what people say they all like fair and sincere praise.

Training and Educating Good People -
Common Sense Tip #10 – People and organizations either learn and grow or they stagnate and die. There is no in-between. Once you take the hill you need to secure your position and move on to the next hill. If you try to just stay on top of the first hill eventually someone will find a way to knock you off.

The Foundation: Establishing Trust -

Common Sense Tip #11 – If people don't trust you the game is over. They won't believe what you say and you can't tell whether what they are saying is what they really feel or what they think you want to hear. If you are at this point you better figure out how to change it or figure out how to start over someplace else.

The Engine of Productivity: Creating Empowerment -

Common Sense Tip #12 – When a team or an individual attempts something new the organization learns whether the attempt is a success or a failure. If people continue to do only what they know is safe and will work, they inevitably will fall further and further behind the competitors who do extend themselves to try knew things. Inaction results in certain failure – there is nothing worse!

The Fuel for Success: Insuring Good Communications -

Common Sense Tip #13 – Don't you know from your own experiences with your family and your friends that you are always anxious to do your best for people that you are close to and that you enjoy working with and being around. Doesn't it just make sense that it would be the same with the people that you work with?   Sure they will work for financial rewards and advancement, but if they are also working because they enjoy and respect the people that they are working with, they will just naturally do better.

The Road to Real Improvement: Enabling Change -

Common Sense Tip #14 – Change isn't all that scary if you are all in it together. Most people are more than willing to explore new things along with a group of friends even though they would be reluctant to try them on their own.   It is the same in business – implement change together as a team and it will produce amazing results and people will embrace it not fear it.

Processes -

Common Sense Tip #15 – No company can afford to have people spend their time figuring out how to do things that others have long since determined the best way to do. So use process to get the easy stuff out of the way and personal creativity to make a difference. Once you figure out the best way to balance your checkbook you wouldn't try a new way each time just to exert your creativity.

The "Gimmee" of Process: Eliminating Waste -

Common Sense Tip #16 – Try doing a time study on yourself every year or so. (By the way that just means keep track of how much time you spend on each task during a day.) A lot of you won't want to take the time to do this or will think that it is silly. However, I did this every two or three years throughout my career and always found the information to be highly revealing. I was always able to look at the way I was spending my time and identify ways to eliminate things that just didn't produce much value. Like everyone else you are probably wasting 20%, 30% or even 40% of your time. So maybe you will agree that it is worth an investment of a few minutes of your time on a study that might save you at least an hour a day from then on?

Common Sense Tip #17 – If you treat people like they can't be trusted then they will behave that way. And if you treat people like they can be trusted then they will prove you right. Which way would you rather be treated?

Common Sense Tip #18 – If you want to try out the effects of a new drug you test it on fruit flies or mice, not elephants. By using fruit flies you can see the effect on 100 future generations in a year whereas you wouldn't even have the second generation of elephants at the end of the year. In other words, if you act quickly, then assess the effectiveness of your actions, and then act again you are a lot better off than if you spend a huge amount of time on your first effort and find out it didn't work the way you wanted it to. You might not ever get enough energy to even start the second effort.

Common Sense Tip #19 – if you are dieting and you weigh yourself every day it isn't really very important whether your scale is in exact alignment with your doctor's scale. What is important is that if your scale tells you that your weight is going down, it really is! What I am trying to say is that most of the time the exact measurement isn't as important as the trend.

The Natural Result of Process: Enabling Change -

Common Sense Tip #20 – It should be clear that you are better off with ten good ideas that are quickly dispersed throughout your company than with 50 good ideas that are selfishly hoarded within a single department. Not only will the ten ideas result in improvements throughout the organization but they will also continue to foster an environment that nurtures good ideas and trust between all employees and departments. The ten good ideas will surely spawn additional thinking as they are understood by others throughout the organization, which will result in the birth of even more good ideas. While the ideas hoarded in one department will only spawn mistrust.

Common Sense Tip #21 – Isn't it pretty clear that whether you are trying to achieve small incremental changes or large revolutionary changes that they are going to be a lot easier to sell in small chunks. We have at least 50 clichés to remind us of this. For example: The longest journey begins with a single step.

Appendix B
A Reading List

Obviously there are hundreds of business books that are well worth reading. This list is not intended to be comprehensive in any way. These are just a few of the books that I remember from over the years as being both enjoyable and thought provoking.

In Search of Excellence by Thomas J. Peters and Robert H. Waterman, Jr., March, 1984

A classic business book that provides insights into the business practices that established certain companies as America's best run and most admired organizations.

Quality is Free by Phillip B. Crosby, April, 1985

One of the many quality books published in this period. This was the approach used by Chrysler Corporation. Crosby argues convincingly that quality doesn't have to be painful.

Competing Against Time by George Stahl and Thomas M. Hout, February, 1990

These authors argue that a company needs to focus on a single element of success. They feel that time is the most critical of these elements and that if you can improve in this area improvements in quality and cost will automatically follow.

Reengineering the Corporation by Michael Hammer and James Champy, 1993

A classic business book that introduced the concepts of re-engineering and literally changed the way that management looked at improving their companies.

The Fifth Discipline Field Book by Peter M Senge, Art Kleiner, Charlotte Roberts, Richard B. Ross and Bryan J. Smith, 1994

An extraordinary compilation of ideas about how to make every aspect of business more effective and productive.

The Discipline of Market Leaders by Michael Treacy and Fred Wiersma, 1995

This books describes the need for companies to identify and focus on their core competencies if they ever hope to succeed in their markets.

Built To Last by Jim Collins, December, 1996

A statistical analysis of the surprising elements that separate great companies from not so great companies. And there are only a few companies that actually make the grade as a great company.

The Dilbert Principle by Scott Adams, 1996

You should read this just to add some humor to your business perspective. But you will also find many insights into why business isn't always very effective.

The Circle of Innovation by Tom Peters, 1997

An amazing book with an innovative idea on every page – unlike almost anything else you are likely to read.

Surfing the Edge of Chaos by Richard Tanner Pascale, Mark Milleman and Linda Gioja, October, 2000

An analysis of why we have to learn to prepare for drastic change. The premise of this book is that unless companies exist on the edge of new developments they will not survive changes when they come.

From Good to Great by Jim Collins, October, 2001

The follow on book to **Built to Last** defines the critical factors that defined the tiny number of companies that have progressed from being good companies to qualifying as great companies.

Managing in the Next Society by Peter Drucker, 2002

No collection is complete without at least one book from the creator of Management Science, Peter Drucker.

And finally

Pooh on Management by Roger E. Allen, 1994

Just because my kids gave it to me. Enjoy!

Appendix C

Bibliography

1   Exley, H. *The Best of Business Quotations.* Waterford, UK, Exley
     Publications Ltd., 1993, Pg. 41

2   Ibid: Pg. 43

3   Ibid: Pg. 59

4   Detroit Free Press Interview for Detroit Magazine, Sunday,
     April 27, 1986

5   Detroit Free Press Interview for Detroit Magazine, Sunday,
     April 27, 1986

6   Iacocca L. *Iacocca an Autobiography.* New York, Bantam Books
     November, 1984

7   Friedman, S. *Smart Cookies Don't Crumble.* New York, G.P.
     Putnam's Sons, 1985, Pg. 210

8   Brainyquotes.com, American Economist Quotes

9   Friedman, S. *Smart Cookies Don't Crumble.* New York, G.P.
     Putnam's Sons, 1985, Pg. 210

A Few Words about the Author

Paul Anders graduated from the University of Michigan with degrees in the unlikely combination of Physics and Economics. He received his MBA at Wayne State University in Detroit and attended the Advanced Management Program at Northwestern's Kellogg School of Business. He spent over 30 years in the business world with the last 14 years being at the Officer level in first the 4th largest non-banking Financial Company in the United States and then at the 8th largest combined gas and electric Utility Company in the United States. He has spoken at various conferences and chaired the industry technical committees for both the American Financial Services Association and the Edison Electric Institute. He has been involved in the implementation of almost every business practice popularized in the last two decades including Total Quality Control, Empowerment, Process Redesign, and the Learning Organization. He has recently retired and now lives with his wife of 43 years in their home in Southeastern Michigan.